T0343526

Also by Joe Dunthorne

Submarine
Wild Abandon
The Adulterants
O Positive: Poems

Children
of Radium

A BURIED INHERITANCE

JOE DUNTHORNE

SCRIBNER

New York   Amsterdam/Antwerp   London
Toronto   Sydney/Melbourne   New Delhi

Scribner
An Imprint of Simon & Schuster, LLC
1230 Avenue of the Americas
New York, NY 10020

This is a work of nonfiction. Some names have been changed.

Originally published in Great Britain in 2025 by Hamish Hamilton,
an imprint of Penguin Books

First Scribner hardcover edition April 2025

For information about special discounts for bulk purchases, please contact Simon &
Schuster Special Sales at 1-866-506-1949 or business@simonandschuster.com.

The Simon & Schuster Speakers Bureau can bring authors to your live event. For more
information or to book an event, contact the Simon & Schuster Speakers Bureau at
1-866-248-3049 or visit our website at www.simonspeakers.com.

Interior design by Hope Herr-Cardillo

Manufactured in the United States of America

10   9   8   7   6   5   4   3   2   1

Library of Congress Cataloging-in-Publication Data is available.

ISBN 978-1-9821-8075-1
ISBN 978-1-9821-8077-5 (ebook)

Image Credits: Page 1 courtesy of Wikimedia Commons; page 59 reproduced by
permission of Steffen Schellhorn; page 87 reproduced by permission of Koç University—
VEKAM Archive; page 119 reproduced by permission of the Political Archive of the
Federal Foreign Office; page 137 courtesy of the author; page 169 reproduced by
permission of the Ida Seele Archive; page 179 courtesy of Munich City Archives; pages
194 and 196 courtesy of the Leo Baeck Institute; page 203 courtesy of the author

Material from chapters I, II, and VIII first appeared in *Granta* magazine, issue 152,
under the title "Daughter of Radium."

This book is for my mother

"Is the invisible visible?"

Interview with Wilhelm Röntgen
following his discovery of X-rays in November 1895

Contents

I.

Perpetual Sunshine

1.

My grandmother grew up brushing her teeth with radioactive tooth-paste. The active ingredient was irradiated calcium carbonate and her father was the chemist in charge of making it. Even before it was available in shops he brought tubes home to his family. Under the brand name Doramad, it promised gums "charged with new life energy" and a smile "blindingly white." Their apartment was so close to the factory that she fell asleep listening to the churning of the autoclave. When they were forced to leave Germany in 1935, they took tubes of it with them, their suitcases gently emitting alpha particles as they traveled a thousand miles east. During the war, she learned that the toothpaste her Jewish father helped create had become the preferred choice of the German army. A branch factory in occupied Czechoslovakia ensured that the troops pushing eastward, brutalizing and murdering, burning entire villages to the ground, could do so with radiant teeth.

Not that she ever told me this. What I knew about my grand-mother's life had all come secondhand, anecdotes worn smooth with each retelling. When my mother gave me a ring for my wedding she told me it had "escaped the Nazis" in 1935. I looked at the oval bloodstone, black with flecks of red, picturing their getaway with the unique clarity of someone untroubled by having done any research. It was my uncle who gave me a poster of the smiling, yellow-haired Doramad girl, glowing from the inside. I pinned it above my desk and began to write about my grandmother's childhood. The project was going well—until an intervention from the person whose actual life it was.

I tried to interview my grandmother at her home in Edinburgh. This was more than a decade ago. Sitting in a low chair, wearing a fuzzy woolen sweater that made her seem out of focus, she let me know that I was not ready. Whatever questions I asked were not the right ones and I remember her yawns becoming increasingly aggressive until at last she said, "Look, why don't you just read a book about it?" Some months later, I tried once more, explaining that I *had* now read a book about it—an award-winning and nuanced cross-generational memoir about a wealthy Jewish family's persecution and migration from Odessa to Vienna to Paris, a masterpiece of the form and perhaps a template for how to approach her own life story, and which it turned out she had already read and hated. She handed it straight back, saying, "No, it wasn't like that." So what *was* it like? I didn't dare ask again.

A part of me imagined that one day near the end she might take my hand and start talking, unburden herself, the decades falling away—and that would be a sign to reach for my notebook. Instead there was slow-creeping dementia and, with it, depression. She had always been funny and honest and even when that honesty tipped into cruelty she used to get away with it because she laughed often with her head thrown back. But now she stopped laughing and started to burn through carers at the rate of one a week, could bring them to tears on their first visit. Her Scottish-German accent gave her put-downs a special power—and she could be just as hard on herself. "Some people are awful kind," she told me once as I pushed her wheelchair through the park. "And some people are like me, awful."

She died in 2017 at the age of ninety-two. At her memorial, my sister and I gave a joint speech in which we tried to re-create her idiosyncratic phrases, a mix of Scots and Bavarian, flashes of Turkish. We'd written to friends and family, and while they all agreed she had said unforgettable things, no one could remember what they were—apart from a handful of insults deemed too gritty for the ceremony. It felt as though we'd only managed to reveal how much of her was missing. That was evocative in its own way. We felt her presence in the lack of it.

It wasn't until two years after her death, during a family get-together, that I ventured into her old bedroom. I would like to say I started nosing around in order to feel close to her again, but the truth was probably nearer to the opposite. It was only now she was gone I felt able to ask more questions about her life, safe in the knowledge she would not answer back. I knew that somewhere in her room was a collection of documents known as "the family archive." I imagined a crumbling bundle of letters hidden beneath a loose floorboard, but found a drawer neatly labeled with a luggage tag: *family archive*. Lined with faded orange wallpaper, it contained war medals, diplomas, antique coins, her father's unpublished memoir, box files of letters in handwriting that leaned almost horizontal, various recorded interviews with my grandmother, an embarrassing folder of my own poems that I had solemnly presented to her when I was a teenager, and a handwritten "recipe" for radioactive toothpaste from November 1925 when she was one year old, her teeth just coming in.

I laid out all the documents on her bed, feeling her disapproval emanate from the walls. It had not escaped my attention that, of my siblings and cousins, I alone was never asked to join her on one of her trips back to Germany, where she was invited several times as a guest of honor by the city of Berlin. Both my sisters reported back on emotionally profound stays, receiving the city's warm yet respectful welcome, being guided from door to door by bilingual hosts with a deep sensitivity to history. Also, luxury hotels with international breakfasts that wrapped all the way round the morning room. It's not as though I was the only one angling for a story. My eldest sister made sketches for a graphic novel, while my filmmaker cousin, Charlie, tracked my grandmother through the city with a DSLR and a handheld microphone. I couldn't help but feel it was a personal snub.

I picked up the heaviest document, *The Memoirs of Siegfried Merzbacher*—her father—which I knew was the foundational text of our family history. In the black-and-white photo on the cover, the chemist behind Doramad toothpaste looked jolly and relaxed, a stack of documents under one arm and luxurious bags under his eyes. My mum and her siblings had only happy memories of their grandpa who they described as warm, soft, "grandpa-ish" and "totally benign." I flicked through his unpublished and unpublishable block of A4 pages, renowned among my relatives largely because so few of us had managed to read it. Even my dad, the most studious person

I know—a historian of the seventeenth-century Dutch empire—
thought it "a bit of a slog" and admitted that he'd skimmed it. And
this was the heavily abridged English translation—five hundred and
nineteen pages, single-spaced. No one still living had got through
the German original: nearly two thousand typewritten pages.

I knew my great-grandfather had worked on his memoir for the
last decade or so of his life, tapping away while smoking thousands
of unfiltered cigarettes. He was still adding footnotes—clarifying
details about his scientific work with numerous carcinogens—when
he died, surprising no one, of cancer. That was in 1971. The foot-
high stack of pages then remained in his son Eugen's office for the
next forty years, unread and emitting low-level guilt among his
descendants, who understood they should definitely take an interest.
It wasn't until Eugen was in his nineties and living in a retirement
community that he decided to abridge the memoir and translate
it so that the younger, English-speaking generations could also feel
bad about not reading it. After working on his translation every day
for two years, Eugen drove to a copy shop to get it printed and died
a week later. And so, holding this spiral-bound document in both
hands, I knew that it was half a century in the making, an end-of-
life project for two generations of my family—and this may explain
why I immediately put it down again.

I started instead by working through my grandmother's interviews. There were four hours with the Anne Frank Center, a short
BBC documentary about German Jews living in Scotland, footage
from a project called *Refugee Voices*, and an unreleased audio recording. She rarely enjoyed being interviewed but, in this last one, she
sounded especially sour. The interviewer's questions kept circling two

years in particular—and I could guess why. 1935 was when she and her family fled to Turkey, leaving behind most of their belongings and their money tied up in blocked bank accounts; 1936 was when they came back with a plan. Under the cover of the Summer Olympics in Berlin they conducted a heist on their own home.

My grandmother was twelve years old. Bunting lined the streets, each individual cobblestone gleamed, and even the city's construction sites had been beautified, their garlands of oak leaves doused in chemical preservative to keep them looking healthy throughout the Olympic fortnight. Goebbels called it a "festival of joy and peace." It was reported that mosquitoes had been completely eradicated from the athlete's village and, instead, the lake was now populated with two hundred storks. Berlin was smiling so hard you could hear its teeth squeak.

Each day my grandmother's parents withdrew the maximum daily allowance from their bank and spent it with the abandon of knowing it would likely get confiscated at the border. At Wertheim's department store, my grandmother got a new violin and her older brother a Leica camera, which he slung around his neck. Eugen was fifteen and already expressing sophisticated opinions about coffee and cigarettes. As they walked down Kurfürstendamm, voices reached them from the trees. Loudspeakers hidden in the branches announced the latest from the stadium. *Attention! Attention! Germany takes gold in the women's javelin . . .*

Her father drove them out to their old apartment in Oranienburg, a small town on the edge of Berlin. He was a fifty-three-year-old chemist who smoked so much that the whole right-hand side of his mustache had turned the color of rust. They were relieved to find the key still turned in the lock. Stepping lightly up the staircase, they were careful not to knock against the banisters and disturb their former neighbors. My grandmother crawled into the thick air of the attic and passed down photographs, letters, jewelry, and a tray of antique coins, all of which were quietly carried downstairs, past the eye peering from a crack in the second-floor door, out to the street, where the car was waiting.

She watched from the back seat as her father steered them south through the center of Berlin, past gliding yellow trams, sports fans with flags around their shoulders, and the rows of long swastika banners that led toward the stadium—the whole street turned red, like staring down a throat—at the sight of which her father's driving became suddenly self-conscious, each corner taken with elaborate care, and it was only many hours later that she, her family, and an unusually heavy briefcase were waved across the border into Czechoslovakia.

At least that's how I understood it, having listened to my family's stories and added a little color of my own. But now I heard the interviewer pressing my grandmother for details. Did she feel threatened or scared? Did they witness or experience any antisemitism? Could she offer more specifics? She recognized the tone of someone digging for trauma and her voice hardened, but still he persevered. Eventually she did offer more details, but they were not ones I was expecting.

They had, she explained, traveled to and from Germany on the *Orient Express*—"two days and two nights of eating." This was the first moment when I sensed my version of events coming under threat from facts. Most of their belongings had already gone with them to Turkey in 1935, she continued, including a Bechstein grand piano, and what they left behind in Berlin was all in storage. When they returned in the Olympic summer, they stayed for a full five weeks, mostly to spend time with relatives. They had French lessons with a teacher who opened the door each day and said: "Children, would you like a pretzel?" There was no heist on their own home, no getaway car, no race to the border. It wasn't even clear if they visited their old apartment. It was true about the blocked bank accounts, the camera, and the violin, but not much else. Her description most resembled a summer holiday. When the interviewer finally said he had no more questions, her chair scraped back and she said, "Oh, thank God."

What made listening to this even worse was that the interrogator was me. This was the interview from 2012, the one where she told me to read a book about it, which I had taped but had never actually played back—for understandable reasons. The recording began with my grandmother halfway through a sentence while I fumbled with the Dictaphone. "Sorry," I said, interrupting, "I realized it wasn't on. Who . . . who . . . who committed suicide?" What followed was a master class in incompetence, an interview so embarrassing that, even now, I could only listen to it for a few seconds at a time, pausing regularly to do breathwork. It was easy to see why I had given up on the idea of writing about her. What was harder to comprehend was how I had managed to forget most of what she actually told me, and work my way back to the story I preferred to believe in.

It was then I started reading my great-grandfather's memoir, hoping to replace my comforting fantasy with something meaningful and true. All that week—as my nephews ran shrieking up and down the long corridor—I slowly worked my way through it. There were a hundred pages of ancestral history, reaching way back to Jizhak Merzbacher, an eighteenth-century trader of animal hides from northeast Bavaria. There were another hundred about Siegfried and his two sisters' unhappy childhood in Munich, during which his Orthodox parents outsourced their affection to a live-in nanny, and he tried to build a perpetual motion machine using nothing more than paper, string, glue, and marbles. After that was an in-depth account of his university studies, early academic career, and the myriad world-changing scientific breakthroughs he very nearly but definitely had not made. Nylon, chlorophyll, various holes in the periodic table he failed to fill. Having been taught by some of the greatest minds of the golden age of German science—Nobel laureates on every page—he ended up brewing vats of headache pills in a converted farmhouse.

Four hundred pages into the memoir, I had only just reached the point at which my grandmother was in the womb. Her father was then forty years old and finally had a job he was proud of, working for the famous Berlin company, the Auergesellschaft, whose gently radioactive streetlamps gave the city its characteristic glow. The Auerlicht burned cleaner and longer because the mantles were soaked in radioactive thorium. In the 1920s, his bosses wanted to expand their range of radioactive products. Other companies were already producing radioactive face cream, radioactive hair tonic, and an energy drink called Radithor, distilled water combined with radium-226 and -228, which was promoted as a source of "perpetual sunshine." Even products that were not remotely radioactive—like lingerie made from "radium silk"—traded on the idea that radium was a miracle cure and the source of mysterious powers. It didn't seem to matter that many of the pioneering radiologists—after years of unprotected contact with a range of radioisotopes—were now dying of their research.

Siegfried was assigned to develop a toothpaste and threw himself into his work. When he developed a persistent dental abscess he saw it as an opportunity. Peeling back his upper lip, he let a colleague inject his upper gums with radium-228 and its daughter, actinium-228. He went home from work with his whole mouth swollen and throbbing but, after two days, the abscess abruptly ruptured, drained, and the infection cleared up. With firsthand proof of the healing properties of radiation, he brought home tester tubes of Doramad to his pregnant wife and son. My grandmother's first experience of irradiated calcium carbonate was via amniotic fluid. She was born on April 14, 1924, happy and healthy, the "hoped-for little girl." They named her Dorothea.

I kept checking the page numbers, trying to work out how Siegfried was going to fit in a full and satisfying account of her childhood, the country's descent into totalitarianism, raising a Jewish family in the Third Reich, escaping to Turkey, the 1936 Olympics—and the war. Instead, reading the final chapter seemed to be another case of *Why don't you just read a book about it?* There was no mention of their escape from—or return to—Germany, heroic or otherwise. He managed to say little about their firsthand experience of persecution and, even when he did, one of his tics was that he invariably followed difficult episodes with soothing memories of a holiday. No sooner had he recalled a train journey to Berlin in 1933, when he was "too cowardly" to say anything as a uniformed man dragged a polite and quiet "Jewish-looking" gentleman out of the carriage, than he was drawn back four decades to 1893, age ten, traveling with his family to the coast at Blankenberge in Belgium, where he saw—for the first time—the "infinite extension" of the sea. If a single sentence could sum up his approach it was: "From this unpleasant subject I now return to my childhood vacations."

It was only at the very end of the manuscript that I understood why he had been dragging his feet. Because if he had written about their life under the Nazis, he would also have needed to write about his new work colleagues after 1933. It turned out that the memoir was, in one sense, an extended confession. Or, more accurately, it was five hundred and six pages of clearing his throat—then thirteen pages of saying it. The memoir culminated with an admission that he had betrayed his "most sacred principles" and never recovered from the guilt.

At this point I realized I would not be writing primarily about my grandmother—and she would at least have been pleased about that.

II.

Super Lost

1.

The yard behind Siegfried's factory was stacked high with fragrant piles of apricot and peach stones, coconut and almond shells. It was July of 1926 and, after proving his talents with radioactive toothpaste, Siegfried had been offered a promotion to the protection department. Day and night, his assistants shoveled fruit pits and nut shells into a rotating furnace and, for the first time in his career, Siegfried felt he was doing something valuable. They were making activated charcoal, nicknamed "the universal antidote" because of its miraculous power to eliminate poisons. With its porous, honeycomb structure, it could suck in toxins and trap them there. A few teaspoons of black powder in a gas-mask filter enabled a man to walk calmly into a room full of chlorine gas.

The only downside to Siegfried's new role was that it brought him in contact with the military. Still he told himself that his research would ultimately save lives. Plus the wages were better and he now had a generous life insurance policy. If he had an accident while testing the filters against the latest chemicals, his family would be well compensated. He and his wife, Lilli, were well aware that the recent years of hyperinflation had wiped out all their savings. She came from a Jewish banking family whose financial prudence had skipped a generation: her father had obliterated her inheritance by investing it all in government bonds. In fact, Lilli and Siegfried worried so much about their finances that their son's first "clearly understandable words" had been "dollar" and "Stresemann"—as in Gustav, the German chancellor. One Christmas Siegfried's bonus had been paid in the stable currency of potatoes. Ever since then, he had become an obsessive and meticulous bookkeeper—recording every item of income and expenditure to two decimal points. So he was minutely attuned to the benefits of a pay rise.

Testing the filters could mostly be done in the relative safety of the laboratory, with a Stufenphotometer and an exhaust hood. Nevertheless it was sometimes deemed necessary for the chemists to undertake field tests. In his first week, he'd watched a young colleague demonstrate the effects of oxygen deprivation and nitrogen narcosis. Wearing a tightly fitted full face gas mask, the chemist had run up and down the corridor, slowly using up his oxygen supply. Eventually, he stopped responding to questions and moments later dropped to the floor. He lay there, unmoving. Siegfried thought he was dead but, when they pulled off the mask, he sat up as though waking from a nap.

As the division's new supervisor, Siegfried felt a certain pressure to volunteer. This was how he came to be sitting on a bench in a sealed tank alongside four colleagues. They wanted "to see how the rising concentration of carbon dioxide and moisture affected our breathing." Presuming that they stayed calm and took steady breaths, which he was trying to do, they should feel no more uncomfortable than they would in a stuffy meeting room. Three other chemists peered in at them through a porthole of inch-thick glass.

He should have mentioned that he was prone to bouts of lightheadedness—had once fainted while climbing the stairs to his apartment—but he didn't want to seem feeble. Looking out at the faces of Dr. Neumann, Herr Worbs, and Dr. Friess, he saw their mouths moving, but couldn't hear them.

Siegfried opened the pad on his lap and, with his pencil, made notes in Gabelsberger, an elegant shorthand in which each word was reduced to a single swirl, a little firework. The atmosphere in the tank was muggy, but he felt fine. Forty minutes later, he made another note, acknowledging the headache that was steadily knuckling the back of his forehead. Closing his eyes for a moment, he wondered whether it was irresponsible for a father of two to take part in this experiment. What was more damaging: agreeing to gently suffocate or refusing to take part and perhaps putting his job at risk? He was always conscious of stereotypes about Jews that needed disproving. It had been the same during the war. People said that Jews got all the cushy noncombat roles, the office jobs, and sent everyone else to choke to death in the trenches. As soon as he heard that rumor, he immediately reported to his superiors and asked to be sent into the field. He recalled his first lieutenant calmly pointing out that what really mattered was finding the role that best suited the individual and, in his case, that was secretarial work. The lieutenant managed to say this without sounding patronizing, not that it stopped Siegfried from feeling judged. That night in the barracks with the other reserves, after Siegfried fell asleep on his inflatable pillow, his comrades deflated it.

He looked through the porthole at his colleagues, trying to read their lips as they spoke. Most of them were good people, he thought. Herr Worbs was a fellow Social Democrat, and they occasionally saw each other at meetings. Dr. Neumann seemed liberal, if not card-carrying. Dr. Friess he was less sure about. He treated Siegfried as a subordinate, but there was no reason to think that was down to anything more than just standard arrogance.

After more than two hours, Siegfried's feet started to prickle, so he rocked them back and forth. He made a note of it in his pad and saw that his Gabelsberger had started to lean. His breath was shallow. He stamped his feet. All three colleagues were watching now. In Herr Worbs's narrowing eyes he noted concern; Dr. Friess's breath misted the glass and he wiped it away with the sleeve of his lab coat. Siegfried's pencil clattered to the floor. When he bent down to pick it up, his vision swam. A moment later he was sitting on the ground. He looked up at his colleagues and they looked down at him.

Siegfried was not asked to be a test subject again—nor did he volunteer. Instead, he focused on evaluating the gas masks in laboratory conditions. This was also dangerous work, but at least he was in control. Every week they tested the filters to see how long they could hold out against phosgene, sulfur mustard, chlorine, and hydrogen cyanide.

The masks had to meet strict military standards, a fact that Siegfried was reminded of each morning when his two bosses arrived from the head office in Berlin. Professor Karl Quasebart was tall, bald, and opulently jowled. He was known among colleagues for his "extraordinarily favorable" relationship with the military. His right-hand man was Dr. Hermann Engelhard, younger, clean shaven, but equally well connected. In 1928 they introduced Siegfried to their latest project.

A secret laboratory for the development of new chemical weapons was being built beside the river. It was funded by the military, but would be designed and run by Auer. And since Siegfried had already become an expert in defending against poisons, he had also, inevitably, become an expert in their production—and he was asked to be the director.

He took a week to give his answer, during which time he and Lilli went on vacation. They left their young children with his sister so that it was just the two of them in Vienna, walking the wide streets and splashing out on dinner at the famous Meissl & Schadn. Across the heavy tablecloths, they discussed the Geneva Convention, the limits of military readiness, and the relative ethics of different kinds of killing while choosing from the menu's twenty-four subtly distinct varieties of boiled beef.

Siegfried knew that making chemical weapons was in clear violation of Article 171 of the Treaty of Versailles: "The use of asphyxiating, poisonous or other gases and all analogous liquids . . . their manufacture and importation are strictly forbidden in Germany." According to Siegfried's memoir, they had "no plans whatsoever to produce these substances industrially or keep them in stock," but simply wanted to be well prepared in case they *might* later decide to. They wanted to be ready—in the event of another war—to manufacture poisons on a massive scale. It was, in his understatement, "a ticklish question" as to whether this already violated the Treaty of Versailles. His older sister's husband—a lawyer who he considered "one of the most principled and honest people I have ever known"—

said he should accept the directorship because otherwise they would just find a different chemist with fewer scruples. By this rationale, he could even frame his decision as ethical. Siegfried also reasoned that every new weapon must have seemed monstrous and evil at first—when the bow and arrow met the gun, when the gun met the bomb—but, in time, medical and defensive technologies always catch up. Surely a death by chemicals was no worse, perhaps kinder, than death by shrapnel? Was the hissing of a gas canister inherently less noble than explosives falling from the sky?

Siegfried also knew he would get to design the apparatus to his own specifications, which was something he'd longed for, having spent the first decade of his career in laboratories that were hardly worth the name. Instead, this would be well funded and prestigious, at least in certain circles. Plus he was already forty-five years old, his hairline in retreat, and he wondered how many more opportunities like this he would have.

Finally he thought of Fritz Haber, the Nobel Prize–winning German-Jewish chemist, an undoubted genius, and one of Siegfried's heroes. Although he had won the Nobel for his invention of synthetic fertilizer—which revolutionized commercial farming, saving millions from hunger—that was soon overshadowed by Haber's second innovation. On a sunny spring afternoon in 1915, he successfully executed the first instance of gas warfare. The French troops near Ypres in Belgium watched a thick green mist approaching from the enemy trenches. That they tried to shoot at it indicates how little they understood what was about to happen. The mist came nearer, carried by the wind, and they noted a peppery smell. Birds dropped from the trees and the grass changed color. When the mist filled their lungs, the soldiers fell to the ground, clawing at their throats and faces, beginning to suffocate on their own mucus. A German soldier approaching the scene an hour later, wearing a gas mask, reported that: "Nothing was moving and nothing was alive. All of the animals had come out of their holes to die. . . . When we got to the French lines the trenches were empty but in a half mile the bodies of French soldiers were everywhere."

Haber became an overnight hero at home, while the Allies tried to extradite him as a war criminal—"the father of chemical weapons." Siegfried believed that one day Haber would be vindicated as chemistry would eventually lead to more humane warfare. He imagined a world in which a gas could be developed that would waft across the fields of battle and put the enemy to sleep, as gentle as a lullaby, leaving them unconscious in the mud for long enough to be carried to the prisoner-of-war camps, where they would wake, defeated but unharmed.

After dinner, Siegfried and Lilli went to the theater to watch *Abie's Irish Rose*, Anne Nichols's broad comedy about a Catholic-Jewish interfaith marriage. Though it had been panned by New York critics for stereotypes that were not only lazy but actively offensive—"No author has ever expressed her contempt for the audience in such flagrant fashion"—the public disagreed, and it became, in the words of another critic from the time, "America's favorite comedy. God forbid." It was now traveling the world, particularly popular with exactly those audience members who the critics thought should be outraged. Irish Catholics and Jews, laughing the loudest, had helped make it the longest-running play on Broadway, applauding its message of mutual understanding and its romantic view of warfare: "with the shells bursting, and the shrapnel flying, with no one knowing just what moment death would come, Catholics, Hebrews and Protestants alike forgot their prejudice and came to realize that all faiths and creeds have about the same destination after all." In Vienna, Hans Moser played the scowling Jewish husband, with curly beard and gold-rimmed pince-nez, leaning into the caricature. Siegfried and Lilli were chuckling from the very first scene.

Siegfried accepted his new job and set about ordering equipment for his laboratory on the banks of the river. The building was steel-framed, with shatterproof glass walls and a concrete roof designed to be impervious to fire. When everything was finished, Siegfried's downstairs neighbor and colleague called it, with clear disapproval, "the pleasure palace on the Havel."

The building stood away from the rest of the factory, protected on all sides by a high, barbed-wire fence. It was divided into three large rooms. The frontmost was for diphosgene, the liquid form of phosgene gas, which smelled like musty hay. Nonfatal exposure could cause chronic bronchitis or emphysema. If inhaled in higher quantities, it eventually flooded its victims' lungs with their own "frothy sputum" so that they drowned from the inside, still conscious. At the end of each day, he and his colleagues would weigh the sample, inspect it for purity, then pour it into the soft earth by the river, the same water in which Siegfried's children sometimes swam, albeit upstream. He was confident that the chemical would be quickly neutralized. "It's possible that the fish felt something," he wrote, "but I doubt it."

The middle room was for diphenyl arsine chloride—aka Clark I—a vomiting agent that the army called the *Maskenbrecher*. It was developed to penetrate gas-mask filters and make the wearer sneeze or cough or vomit and, as a result, take off their masks so that more serious poisons could go to work. (In 1917, another of Fritz Haber's innovations had been to combine Clark I and diphosgene into one weapon, the former intended to make the enemy tear off their masks so that the latter could enter the lungs.)

But the most dangerous work took place in the back room, closest to the river, where the apparatus was kept behind a sealed glass wall. Siegfried and his colleagues had to reach in through narrow hatches. Part of what made sulfur mustard so risky was its apparent harmlessness. The color and texture of olive oil, it smelled like garlic and absorbed rapidly into the skin with no more than a faint itching. Victims could unknowingly receive high doses and only days later see their red patches of skin develop into massive pus-filled blisters that, in turn, took months to heal and often became infected. If droplets of sulfur mustard entered the lungs, it burned its victims from the inside, stripping the nose, throat, and bronchial tubes. During the First World War, military doctors noted the particular hopelessness of soldiers who saw little to no progress in their festering wounds, whose skin was too fragile to be bandaged, and who could not sleep for coughing.

The British called it mustard gas but in Germany, it was called "Lost" after Lommel and Steinkopf, the scientists who first developed a method of large-scale production in 1916. So when Dr. Ulrich Hofmann, a shovel-bearded man from the war department, encouraged Siegfried to improve the recipe by substituting the sulfur with arsenic, Hofmann called this hypothetical new weapon "Super Lost." Siegfried politely pretended that his military colleague understood the finer subtleties of chemistry. Still, that was the nature of Siegried's work and he went about developing an upgrade. His memoir did not offer any details about the success or otherwise of this project. All he noted was that, at the end of each day, the toxic substance was poured into an iron kettle and buried in a deep hole.

He often worried about Lilli and the children living so close to the laboratory—and downwind. Siegfried knew too well that accidents could happen because they were sometimes his fault. Once, while stirring flakes of sodium into an arsenic trichloride solution— trying to make a new vomiting agent—he added too much, too quickly, then heard a hissing noise followed by an explosion. He ran from the room and watched through the glass as the vent sucked out the noxious vapor, releasing it into the air above Oranienburg. Their apartment on Lindenstrasse was a minute's walk away.

While this was a minor incident, Siegfried understood how easily things could escalate. In the spring of 1928, a huge explosion at a rival chemical weapons laboratory in Hamburg had sent a cloud of phosgene drifting across the landscape. The world's press took interest because this was an unsubtle clue about the state of German rearmament. Two fishermen on a nearby canal collapsed and died in hospital. A groundskeeper, his wife, and child all choked to death. In London, the international correspondent for the *Times* described "a plague-stricken area, where men and women, haggard from sleeplessness, walk about haunted by the fear that they will yet be the victims of the invisible peril." Siegfried was well aware of the Hamburg accident because his boss, Dr. Engelhard, published a full analysis, treating it as a helpful bit of field research, establishing the dispersion rate and approximate time of lethal exposure, noting that humans, goats, and rabbits had all been killed "whether they were inside rooms or outside." If a similar accident occurred in the Oranienburg laboratory and the wind carried it west then, according to his colleague's survey, Siegfried's apartment was well within the zone of lethal exposure. One minute would be enough.

At night, where once he lay in bed, eased to sleep by the distant churning of the autoclave, he now stood at his daughter's bedroom door, listening to her breathe.

2.

You could not call any of this a family secret, since it was right here, on very white paper, with half a dozen bound copies distributed among my relatives. And yet I could not recall a time in which anyone had actually mentioned it.

"You must have known," my mother said, before lowering her voice, "about the *chemical weapons*."

Perhaps I had chosen to forget. This, as I was learning, was an inherited talent.

From the doorway my wife, only half listening, looked up. "Sorry. Who was it that made chemical weapons?"

My mother glanced down at Siegfried's photo on the front of his memoir—her grandpa, crinkly eyed and smiling.

"So your grandfather . . . ?"

"Yes."

"But not . . . for the Nazis? Wasn't he Jewish?"

My mother raised her eyebrows and left them there.

I assumed that the next bit of research would be easy: tracking down more evidence of Siegfried's chemical weapons laboratory in

Oranienburg. To be honest, I had expected—in my grandmother's words—to read a book about it. Since it was possible to find two hundred pages about the *Collectible Spoons of the 3rd Reich*, I did not anticipate having to go farther than, at most, the library. But when I spoke to one of the leading experts in the history of German chemical warfare, Dr. Florian Schmaltz, he explained why Oranienburg was a particular problem—and that I should lower my expectations. Many of the official records that might have covered this period had not survived the British and American bombs that ripped through the town on March 15, 1945. Of the records that were not blown up, some were removed to the USSR after the end of the war, as the Red Army planned to build their own atomic bomb. They took away useful technology, documents, and living scientists, a number of whom were forcibly relocated to Moscow. After the Russians it was the Americans' turn. They seized more records, copied some of it to microfilm, but also lost many originals. Then, in 1958, Auer was merged with a US-based defense manufacturer, Mine Safety Appliances, a company which does not seem hugely motivated to maintain a public archive of material that could prove its connection to the Holocaust. Finally there was my own mother, who admitted that, when clearing out my grandmother's flat after her death, she had dumped a large box of Siegfried's letters and documents straight into the recycling.

3.

I managed to convince my wife to join me on what I pitched as a city break with a little light research thrown in. I watched her expression as we took the S-Bahn north, the Berlin skyline slowly giving way to deep forest. As I would learn, there was a reason that Oranienburg had been so popular with military industrialists. It was only half an hour from the city, but felt like another world.

On the day we visited, the southern part of the town was being evacuated because a half-ton Second World War bomb had been found buried in the soft banks of the Havel. The authorities were now lowering the water level to reach it. It was a big operation; a row of pipes like a church organ were slurping at the muddy river. Five thousand people had left their homes, while a hundred police officers and firefighters established the perimeter.

We walked north, away from the cordon and toward the local archive. In a cobblestoned courtyard, we met the archivist, Christian Becker, a tall and cheerful man who had spent twenty-one years attending to Oranienburg's key role in one of the darkest periods of human history. While leading us down into the low-ceilinged basement, he talked about the bomb in the river as we might talk about the weather. We learned that this was the 209th explosive found in this town since German reunification in 1990, and experts estimated that as many as four hundred more remained beneath the ground. One for every hundred residents. He said that whenever there was an evacuation, children were disappointed if they didn't get a day off school.

The problem with the bombs in Oranienburg, Christian explained, was that they had delayed fuses—designed to postpone detonation by a few hours or days in order to cause maximum surprise and havoc. But many of these fuses malfunctioned and ended up working to longer schedules. All the bombs will still go off—but it could be today or fifty years from now. In 2013, a local man returned from walking his dog to find his home blown up, in its place a twenty-meter-wide crater pooling with brown water. This explained why Oranienburg remains the only town in Germany with a dedicated ordnance disposal team actively searching for unexploded bombs. And every few weeks they find one. Through the council's website, local residents can arrange for the removal of garden waste, Christmas trees, and live explosives.

Christian talked us through the many reasons that Oranienburg had been a particular target during the war. It was not just Siegfried's chemical weapons laboratory. Oranienburg was nicknamed "the SS town." Here they had the headquarters that controlled all the concentration camps in Germany. There was also the gas mask factory, in which my great-grandfather worked, as well as a warplane manufacturer, the Sachsenhausen concentration camp, and a secret facility producing uranium oxide for the Nazis' atomic bomb project. This was the quiet town in which Berlin hid its secrets. Even the building we were standing in, a former palace, had been used as barracks by the SS.

When the local people of Oranienburg started to rebuild the town after the war, they filled the numerous bomb craters with whatever material was readily available, which, in this instance, was the tumbling heaps of monazite sand that lay around the grounds of the factory. This was the material from which my great-grandfather and his colleagues extracted radioactive thorium to use in their toothpaste. So now the foundations of Oranienburg were both explosive *and* radioactive. It was not unusual for the bomb disposal team to wear hazmat suits while digging.

Christian didn't have much information about the "pleasure palace on the Havel." This did not seem so surprising now I knew how much else was going on in Oranienburg. But after disappearing into the rows of shelves, he did find a directory of postal addresses from 1931 and was pleased to discover Siegfried's name and an address, Lindenstrasse 15. Before I could ask whether that building still existed, he showed us a large poster pinned to the wall. What resembled the pockmarked surface of the moon was, in fact, a composite of aerial photos of Oranienburg taken shortly after the Allied bombardment of March 1945—when one bomb fell every second for forty-five minutes. Craters showed where they went off and smaller keyhole-shaped openings indicated where they didn't—and where they might still be buried. Christian pointed his finger at a rash of craters and said, "Here's Lindenstrasse."

While I abandoned my hopes of ever standing in my grandmother's childhood bedroom, Christian located an architectural plan of their company-owned apartment block in 1932. Unfolding the crumbly pages revealed a grand three-story corner building with a red-tiled roof, a paneled front door flanked by columns and, most notably, a bomb shelter in the basement. I knew about this from Siegfried's memoir. The shelter was an educational tool, built by his employers in order to provide practical training in preparation for air war. Students at the company's "Gas Protection School" would attend a lecture on the chemistry of poison, then walk to Lindenstrasse, heading down into the basement to role-play the town's destruction. Siegfried and Lilli used to hear the clomping of the students' feet in their hallway as students examined their apartment building, discussing what materials would burn fastest in the event of a firebomb. Apparently there was a promotional photo of my grandmother and her brother inside the air-raid shelter, age eight and eleven—though I couldn't track it down.

———

By the time we emerged from the archive, the protective cordon around the riverbank had been lowered and residents were returning to their homes. Photos on social media showed André Müller, head of the bomb squad, with his hand resting proudly on another deactivated American explosive. It was orange with rust and resembled a whole roast pig, an oilcloth stuffed in its mouth. We watched a video of the mayor handing Müller flowers, thanking him because there was now "one less monster in Oranienburg." Only 399 monsters to go.

Walking back through the quiet streets, we tried not to think about the homes built on radioactive sand or the unexploded bombs that were positioned, nose up, beneath our feet. It didn't help that my wife was pregnant. I thought of Lilli, my great-grandmother, approaching her due date, brushing her teeth with Doramad. Next week we would be going for our "anomaly scan." We envisaged the doctor asking, "So remind me why you spent a long weekend in Germany's most radioactive town?"

We walked to the junction of Lindenstrasse and Lehnitzstrasse, where Siegfried and Lilli's apartment had once stood, and which was now a Park & Ride bus stop. Nearby was a fenced-off area that looked, at first, like an ordinary construction site until we saw the rows of regularly spaced boreholes that meant the bomb squad had been there, searching. We stopped to do some research on our phones. My wife learned that Oranienburg remains a popular weekend destination for the amateur spectrometrist community. They come with Geiger counters and leave with a soil sample. On the pages of Gammaspectacular.com I discovered a link to a survey by the Federal Office for Radiation Protection from 1997. As well as highlighting the places where bomb craters were filled with radioactive monazite sand, it picked out three areas with greatly increased radiation.

"It looks like one of the hot spots is out on the canal at the edge of town," I said. "And the second one is that football pitch we passed earlier."

"And where's the third one?"

I frowned and handed her my phone to see.

We looked down at our feet and then at the nearby construction site. Without a word, we started walking back to the train station.

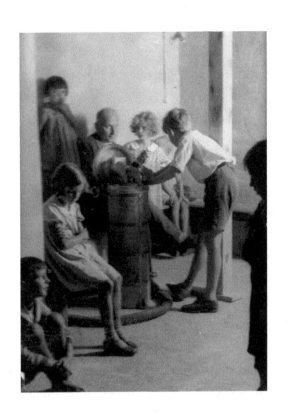

4.

My cousin in America found the photo. It showed my grandmother and her brother in the apartment block's air-raid shelter in 1932. Some of the other children in the scene look somber, arms folded, staring at the floor as though they have been asked to imagine how they would feel if the air in their town became unbreathable. Eugen, age eleven at the time, is cranking the ventilator by hand. My grandmother at eight years old is frizzy-haired and tight-lipped, staring out with a look of disapproval I felt I recognized.

The picture had been part of a photo shoot for *Die Gasmaske*, a trade magazine published by Auer. In his memoir, Siegfried wrote that he and Lilli were not fond of this "propaganda" journal and he made a point of mentioning that he "never wrote an article in it. That wasn't my thing." But they didn't want to seem uncooperative and so the photo was taken and published.

Despite the ominous atmosphere in the picture, my grandmother remembered those years of her childhood as "very free and easy"—cycling, swimming, spending most of her time outdoors. Even in January of 1933, she and her brother were ice-skating on the frozen canal and flatland sledding through the fields outside the town. It wasn't until the end of that month that things started to change. President Hindenburg, eighty-five years old and increasingly senile, appointed a new young chancellor, Adolf Hitler. Though Hindenburg did not like this man or his thuggish party, he believed that—under the steadying influence of other, more experienced cabinet members—he could be "tamed." As the vice-chancellor, Franz von Papen, wrote: "Within two months, we will have pushed Hitler so far into a corner that he'll squeak."

It took less than two days to realize their mistake. In Oranienburg, there was trouble on Bernauer Strasse and Siegfried and Lilli kept their children indoors. The Jewish-owned butchers, Bach Brothers, had its windows smashed. In Berlin, tens of thousands of uniformed members of the SA and SS and *Der Stahlhelm*—an antidemocratic paramilitary group—marched through the Brandenburg Gate, carrying torches, celebrating their arrival in the rooms of power, and singing, *We want to die for the flag*. One newspaper reported that there were no more than 20,000 paramilitaries in the streets while a pro-Nazi publication wrote that, including civilians, 700,000 people had processed through the capital, the huge difference between these numbers indicating a division between two incompatible versions of reality. Some saw the beginning of a national revolution, others saw a few extremists letting off steam.

By April of 1933, a new law limited the number of Jewish children in each school, a rule that did not affect my grandmother because she was already the only Jewish child in her class. Her headmaster, Dr. Katz, went out of his way to promise her that she would be treated no differently than any other child. And yet, by the following year, she had to stand in silence each morning while her fellow students saluted the Führer and sang "these ghastly songs." She sometimes found herself joining in with the milder ones, but only because "the tunes were good."

Lilli and Siegfried enrolled both their children in weekend classes, learning Hebrew at a Jewish school in Berlin, though Siegfried had long ago abandoned his own faith and Lilli's own family had never been practicing. Nevertheless, the whole family celebrated Purim with little Dorothea dressed up as the ancient king of Persia in an ermine gown, with a long white beard. They watched her summon all the wisdom of her nine years and send the Jew-hating Haman to the gallows. They ate soft pastries in the shape of him—plucking out his raisin eyes—in order "to literally consume the evil." Their twelve-year-old son was not convinced. He decided he would not have a bar mitzvah because he knew he would "only do it for the presents."

Meanwhile, around the corner from their apartment, an old brewery had been converted into one of the country's first concentration camps. Like other early camps, the one in Oranienburg was somewhere the National Socialists could lock up their political opponents without warning or reason—under the euphemism of "protective custody." One prisoner, a communist named Willi Ruf, arrived in the camp to discover that one of his jailers was a fascist named Willi Ruf—his father. In the mornings, Siegfried and Lilli were woken by the shuffling footsteps of prisoners being marched past their windows, heading out to dig up tree roots or work on the roads. The camp was near the center of town and open to view from the street. While new prisoners stood for hours in the yard, people walked past with their shopping.

Siegfried and Lilli no longer let their daughter walk around town alone. Throughout Oranienburg, left-wing prisoners from the camp had been forced to scrub left-wing political posters from the walls. Every Sunday afternoon the Merzbachers were visited by Therese, Siegfried's Berlin cousin, whose husband had been the mayor of nearby Luckenwalde. As both a Jew and a Social Democrat, he was among the first to be locked up. Once a week, Therese came to Oranienburg to bring him fresh clothes and talk to him for the allotted thirty minutes, while guards sat beside them, listening. Then she went for tea with the Merzbachers, who, it went unsaid, were also Jewish Social Democrats. In this way, Siegfried spent Sunday comforting his cousin about the brutalities of the state, then Monday with Colonel Moyn at the weapons laboratory. At work, Dr. Engelhard repeatedly reassured Siegfried that he would come to like Hitler eventually. He just needed to "know him better."

Siegfried and Lilli were relieved that their children's school was still flying the black, red, and gold flag of the Weimar Republic. At the parent-teacher association, the headmaster said that he would not take it down at the request of "any association of goatherds." But a few weeks later, a group of those goatherds arrived at the school in SS uniforms, burned the flag, and raised the swastika. This was the moment that their small town became, as Siegfried put it, *ungemütlich*— "uncozy"—and where you might expect his memoir to really start. The military for whom he was developing chemical weapons would, within two years, discharge all Jews from the armed forces, add swastikas to their uniforms and, en masse, swear their "unconditional obedience" to the Führer, an act of voluntary subservience about which even Hitler himself was surprised. And again I found myself reading the final page of the memoir and its two most unconvincing words: *The End.*

5.

It was a strange coincidence that, as I was coming to terms with Siegfried's career in chemical weapons, my mother was putting together our family's application to reclaim German nationality as descendants of victims of Nazi persecution. This was the moment that we became accidental research partners. She would send me letters from the office of Heinrich Himmler, documenting the groundless revocation of Siegfried's citizenship, and I would send her articles about his employers training the SS. She found documentation of the moment when he was given the additional first name Israel—as part of a law to ensure all Jews had Jewish-sounding names and could not hide behind German ones like Siegfried—while I listed which of his colleagues turned up in the Nuremberg trials.

My mum told me that there was nothing ideological about her decision to apply for German citizenship. She said it was mainly just something to keep her busy during retirement. While my father had got big into watercolors, she was seeking formal reconciliation with the country that had tried to systematically eliminate her forebears. We were fortunate that my grandmother had died before we became eligible to apply, so we did not have to hear her opinions about the idea of us becoming "naturalized."

Throughout our research, neither my mother nor I had found any concrete documentation of Siegfried's chemical weapons laboratory, the only detailed mention of which was in his own memoir. This was what led me to the reading room of the Jewish Museum in Berlin.

I watched a tall stack of volumes being wheeled out on a metal trolley. This was the original copy of Siegfried's memoir, eighteen hundred pages in German. The first six volumes looked almost judicial, bound in full-grain leather, but I noticed that the seventh was loose, a pile of thin typewritten paper, the uppermost pages of which had been singed by a flame. Of course I started with these. I then realized that the version of the memoir I had read only had *six* volumes. I checked and double-checked. This explained why it felt incomplete. The English translation was missing the entire final volume—1933 onward.

Looking at where a flame had charred the paper, it now seemed obvious that I had uncovered a major conspiracy, a silence passed down in the bloodline. I sustained this thought for the whole three weeks it took to have the pages translated. It had not occurred to me that Siegfried, a committed smoker and napper, might have nodded off while typing, a lit cigarette dangling in his fingers. I also failed to consider that his son might have edited out these final pages—all one hundred and fifty of them—because they were, after all, quite boring.

On receiving the translation, I read the words: "Before I talk about our experiences at the beginning of the Third Reich, our emigration to Turkey, and my new tasks at the Turkish Red Crescent in Ankara, I'd like to continue with my account of world affairs. . . ." There followed—now for the third time—an in-depth report on the collapse of the Weimar Republic, the rise of extreme left- and right-wing politics, and how that polarization was exploited by the National Socialists. I knew that Siegfried cribbed most of this from the twelve-volume Brockhaus encyclopedia he kept by his side. This did not feel like history so much as graphomania, a pathological need to keep filling the pages, to drown out the silence with the clatter of keys. Every sheet dedicated to, for example, analysis of the London meeting of the Dawes Committee in 1924 was one fewer in which he might recall his colleagues in 1935 or what was buried in the Oranienburg soil. After a hundred and fifty pages of relentless context, he finally returned to the point. "With a heavy heart, I now begin to tell the story of our personal experiences in the last years we spent in Germany, 1933–1935," he wrote, only to immediately apologize because his memory had "suffered greatly" and he was not, after all, able to offer anything of note. He was now in his mid-eighties. The shredding machines of old age had done their work.

With little else to go on, I returned to the documents shared with me by Christian, the archivist in Oranienburg. One of those was a beach towel–sized site plan of all of Auer's properties in the town, dated May 1935—and which he had let me photograph. Now that I had time to examine it more closely I found that, among the dozens of warehouses and workshops, one particular building stuck out. It was labeled *Versuchsfabrik*—experimental factory. This building exactly matched the description in the memoir: three rooms cordoned off by the curve of the river, a short walk from the family apartment on Lindenstrasse. All its parts were marked: glass roof, cobblestone yard, sewage pits, steel girders, shatterproof glass, and an ice cellar. Even though this was the most modest kind of epiphany—a few smudgy line drawings—it was the first time I'd had any verification from a primary source and not a blood relation.

6.

On my second trip to Oranienburg, I went alone but armed with a Geiger counter. I had bought it secondhand on eBay, a little plastic box about the size of a deck of cards and made by a company called Radex. In my backpack, I also had the cheapest trowel I could find in Berlin, a pair of gardening gloves, a teaspoon, and a clip-lock Tupperware, all part of my plan to independently verify which chemicals Siegfried had been working with at his laboratory.

In preparation for this trip, I had spent the previous week carrying the Geiger counter round our house, noting that the shelf where we kept our shampoos, ointments, and sun creams showed a reading twice the level of background radiation. On one occasion my four-year-old son and I took the device over to the hospital across the road and sat on some blue chairs outside the X-ray rooms. We were hoping for what the hobbyists call "scatter," a few rogue rays escaping the machine and finding their way through the wooden door, giving us a pleasing volcano shape on our graph. We waited for the *Do Not Enter* sign to start glowing and, when it did, watched the screen as the number ticked up, then settled at a reading just marginally less radioactive than the shelf in our bathroom. My son, disappointed, stood up and pressed the device flat against the door.

What I learned from this research was that radiation, for the most part, was reassuringly mundane. Though I had been quick to think of its extreme forms—acid fallout, exclusion zones—I was less conscious of its presence in our everyday lives: our microwave's nugget of thorium; the alpha particles emitted by the smoke detector; the quietly radiant bananas in the fruit bowl; or, indeed, the waves emitted by my own body. The people we sleep beside are gently dosing us as they snore. And because it's everywhere, it's hard to find a genuine hot spot, which is part of what makes the search for it addictive. I now understood why there was a whole scene of radiation nerds with their scintillators and ionization chambers, all competing for that rare-frequency spike on the spectrograph. And I also understood why, for certain people, there were few towns more attractive than Oranienburg—a paradise of irradiated subsoil.

From the station, I walked past my family's old address and on toward the bend in the river Havel, holding aloft my Geiger counter. It was mid-July and everyone I passed had ice creams. On my phone I looked at a photo of Auer's site plan from 1935. Switching back and forth between the hand-drawn document and my pegman on Google Maps, I navigated by the curve of the river, slinking into the trees at the edge of the water. I kicked away the dry leaves and started digging. According to my calculations, this was the spot where, from 1928 to 1935, Siegfried came each morning to refine and upgrade a range of poisons and where, each evening, he and his colleagues either buried them, burned them, or poured them into the river.

My breathing grew heavy as I dug, waiting for a smell to hit me, a burning throat or sudden headache. As a security measure, the Geiger counter lay on the ground beside me. Oranienburg had also been a key site in the Nazis' attempts to build an atom bomb. In 2017, a local metal detectorist had happened across a rock with unusual properties and taken it home to show his children. Two days later, his street had been evacuated while government workers took away the radioactive lump in a lead-lined suitcase.

As the hole deepened, my Geiger counter recorded a tangible uplift in combined beta and gamma radiation, though it remained within governmental health limits. I scraped out some soil, transferred it to the Tupperware then refilled the hole. In order to make a representative survey of the area, I conducted five more excavations along the river. Each time I plunged my bright green trowel into the earth, I tried not to think of all the unexploded bombs lying dormant in Oranienburg. Great risks were necessary in the name of groundbreaking research, I told myself. Then I stirred all the samples together with the teaspoon.

I sent the soil away for analysis and, twelve working days later, received the results that told me nothing I couldn't have learned from the state environmental agency or the blogs of intrepid spectrometrists. And the real revelation came, several weeks later, in an unrelated email.

7.

I was back in London when I got the message from Christian. He said he'd uncovered a "little sensation" while looking through old issues of *Die Gasmaske*. This was the industry magazine for which I believed my great-grandfather "never wrote an article"—until Christian told me that he had. He'd found a reference to one written in 1932, though he couldn't find the piece itself because his archive only had an incomplete run of the magazine.

I expected to hunt hard for the missing issues, but the British Library had all eleven volumes available for next-day viewing. In a seat at the back of the reading room, I started at the beginning and worked my way through, from 1929 to 1940. *Die Gasmaske*'s early issues focused on developments in filter technology, a summary of recent deaths by avoidable failures in industrial safety practice, and a letters section with a lively debate about whether cyanide actually smelled of burnt almonds. As though attempting to compensate for the unsettling tone of the magazine, there was also a cheerful "snapshots" section, which tried to capture the lighter side of preparation for chemical and ballistic warfare.

In a 1929 issue, I recognized the Allergolix that Siegfried had given to Lilli to help with her hayfever, a mask so tight it left a textured red indent across her forehead. The picture showed carefree allergy sufferers relaxing with a game of chess and a cutlery catalogue.

In a 1930 issue, there was a photo of Siegfried and his colleagues standing outside the lecture theater of the Gas Protection School. Then, in a 1932 issue, I found the picture of my grandmother and her brother, as children, in the air-raid shelter. I started to feel like I was flicking through a family photo album. I'd seen the air-raid shelter photo before but never in context. The accompanying text explained that, following an act of war, civilians like these would need to gather in an airtight structure, one in which "the doors cannot be opened to latecomers."

I found Siegfried's article in the winter issue of 1932—a carbon monoxide special. His piece—"The Risks of Carbon Monoxide from Combustion Engines"—discussed the growing problem of vehicle pollution in cities. On first look, it was hard to imagine why he would have lied or forgotten about a publication in which he was, in a sense, an early climate scientist, exploring the effect of vehicle pollution on public health.

Then I noticed the article that shared a page with Siegfried's. It was also about carbon monoxide, written by a Dr. Ernst-Robert Grawitz, a name I half recognized. The piece began: "Practical experience always shows that the most severe poisoning occurs when the poisoned person has spent a certain time in a small and securely locked room." The page was illustrated with images of people killed by carbon monoxide exposure, their swollen and blistered hands and feet, skin a ferocious pink. In one photo, a healthy hand was also in frame. The purpose of magazines like these was, in the words of historian Olaf Groehler, to "help large sections of the German people to psychologically familiarize themselves with the horrors of chemical warfare, to get used to the horror."

At the time he published this article, Dr. Grawitz was a respected clinician in a Berlin hospital while already a member of both the National Socialists and the SS. He would go on to become the chief medical officer of the SS, enthusiastically overseeing human experimentation on prisoners and recommending to Himmler the gas chambers as the most effective method of mass killing.

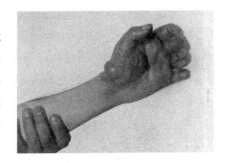

He also organized the gassing—with carbon monoxide from diesel engines—of those patients the Nazis deemed "unworthy of life." He vowed to be the first in line to oversee the execution of the mentally ill and funded programs to eradicate what Himmler called "the perverted world of the homosexual." Near the end of the war in April 1945—having visited Hitler in his bunker for the last time—Grawitz killed himself and his family at their home in Babelsberg. As he sat with his wife and son, he held two grenades in his hands underneath the dining table.

In the steady light of the British Library, I found myself listing the reasons that this was merely circumstantial. Siegfried had no editorial involvement in *Die Gasmaske*. He had nothing to do with commissioning its authors nor did he choose the order in which the articles were published. In 1932 the Nazis were not even in power.

So I carried on reading, watching the tone of the magazine shift. There was a four-page spread about new developments at the Gas Protection School. In September of 1933, they moved to bigger premises and added an airtight "irritant room" for testing exposure to different chemicals, along with trenches in which to re-create attacks under warlike conditions. There was a photo of students learning to maintain a forced march in gas masks and another of right-wing paramilitaries carrying limp bodies across a field for practice. By 1934, one issue featured the hundreds of Auer employees who had joined the National Socialist factory workers' union, the NSBO. Another showed an SS troop being trained at the Gas Protection School.

From 1935, the pages of the magazine reflected a nationwide campaign of military readiness as it became mandatory for every

school to educate students in air and gas protection. Young people learned the chemical structures of common poisonous gases and how they could identify a phosgene attack by the smell of fresh-cut grass.

In the May/June issue of 1935, I was surprised to find a second article by my great-grandfather, a coauthored piece called "The Danger of Carbon Monoxide in Garages." Again, it was an article ostensibly about saving lives—exploring the health risks posed by engine pollution in unventilated spaces—and yet, as with so much in this magazine, it was difficult to set aside the knowledge of what was to come, particularly because Siegfried's coauthor was a party member. Dr. Erwin Thaler had joined the National Socialists two years earlier.

Their article named the specific concentration of carbon monoxide from vehicle exhausts that would, in an enclosed space, cause "considerable symptoms of poisoning." They also noted the relatively mild toxicity of an idling engine—as opposed to one in motion. This was a distinction later exploited in the Nazis' first mass killing technology, the "gas van." These purpose-built vehicles—some of which would be made and tested in Sachsenhausen, the concentration camp just outside Oranienburg—channeled exhaust fumes into airtight cargo compartments so that the dozens of victims could be killed and, if needed, simultaneously driven to the graves in which their bodies were dumped. Hundreds of thousands of people were murdered this way and the gas vans were only discontinued because, among other things, the SS felt the victims moved too slowly through the three stages of poisoning. The sound of their screaming and throwing themselves against the locked doors was found to be upsetting.

8.

I paced in loops around the library's high walkways, repeating my caveats. He only found out after the war that his coauthor was a party member. The relationship between their article and the gas vans was purely speculative, an invention of retrospect. Siegfried immigrated to Turkey five years before the first gas van was put in use.

As I thought this, I kept coming back to Siegfried's claim that he had never written for the magazine at all. *That wasn't my thing.* I wondered if this was outright dishonesty, a trick of memory, or a blend of the two. Perhaps it was a lie so well established that he no longer realized he was telling it. Perhaps, over time, he had not only forgotten about having written for *Die Gasmaske* but had then imagined himself as having been ideologically opposed to doing so. I could hardly judge since my decision to write this book had been premised on my own delusion: that the ring on my finger was heroically smuggled out of the Berlin Olympics, a story that seemed like it *should* be true, regardless of the evidence. Looking back through Siegfried's memoir, I wondered how much of it was his preferred version of the past.

I got in touch with Evonik Industries, a "specialty chemicals company" that is one of the modern-day successors to Auer. As multinational corporations go, they are fairly progressive when it comes to bluntly acknowledging their role in exploiting genocide. They have funded independent research and maintain an archive through which academics can explore the many ways that their various historic subsidiaries benefited from the Third Reich. Though it was easy to be cynical about the underlying profit motive behind this openness, it was still startling to read an acknowledgment on the company's slick website that one of their parent companies, Degussa, knowingly profited from processing gold teeth ripped from the mouths of gassed Jews.

On the phone to Andrea Hohmeyer, one of the Evonik archivists, I told her what I knew about Siegfried, about his articles in *Die Gasmaske*, his colleagues and the chemical weapons laboratory by the river—the one that did not exactly manufacture chemical weapons but researched the best way to do so, hypothetically, should the need arise. She listened to all this and suggested that I look into a town called Ammendorf, a hundred miles southwest of Berlin. She emailed me some documents from the Evonik archive that showed that by 1934 the military and the directors at Auer were planning a factory that was not remotely theoretical—and they had found the perfect location.

I asked my mother if she wanted to join me on the next leg of my research, with her speaking German on my behalf while we explored the still-contaminated grounds of a former chemical weapons plant near Halle in Saxony-Anhalt. We might also, I suggested, make time to admire the ornate Baroque architecture of nearby Leipzig.

"Ah, *Leip*zig," she said, correcting my pronunciation. "Lovely city. But no."

So I traveled alone, taking the train across miles of flatness—fields, farmland, the occasional church spire. In my backpack I had the final few pages of volume six of Siegfried's memoir and an out-of-print book called *The Silent Death* by Olaf Groehler. It was here that I had found further documentation of the Oranienburg laboratory, including an important distinction from how Siegfried presented his work there. In his memoir, Siegfried wrote that he and his colleagues had learned *how* to manufacture and store huge volumes of chemical weapons but, importantly, that there were no plans to put their research into practice. He claimed that the military just wanted to be "well prepared" in the event of war.

In reading *The Silent Death,* however, I understood that this, too, was a selective account. What was true was that Siegfried and his colleagues did not industrially manufacture chemical weapons *in Oranienburg.* Nor did they stockpile them there. What he failed to mention was that, long before the war, his research had been put into action—somewhere else.

Arriving at Halle's glassy modern train station, I hired an e-scooter and headed south, away from the historic market and the famous botanical gardens and toward the outer suburbs. As I passed large out-of-town supermarkets, it was hard to imagine that somewhere underground were the remains of enormous tiled bunkers that had stored thousands of tons of a blistering agent.

I continued scooting south until the cycle path ended and then so did the road, closed for construction. After I spent some time bumping along an unpaved track the scooter started to beep and then stopped abruptly, a mile short of my destination. It had reached an invisible line it refused to cross. I parked it and walked the final stretch down the four-lane highway, semitrucks barreling past. As I perhaps should have guessed, Ammendorf was not an e-scooter kind of place.

III.

Orgacid

1.

The former poison factory had become a nightclub. Covering one side of the brick building was a massive graffitied mural of a red devil, his eyes glowing as he screamed at the sky. While clubbers queued, taking sly dabs of recreational chemicals when the bouncers weren't looking, they could lean against the original tilework engraved with the periodic table.

The club was called Stellwerk—Signal Box—a reference to the nearby railway tracks where the train to Merseburg rattled past every hour. Back in the 1930s, the railway line branched directly into the grounds of the factory, allowing for the easy and discreet delivery of raw materials.

I climbed up a fire escape decorated with palm tree leaves to peer into the rear of the club, an area that the posters called "the beach," but was more accurately an adult sandbox with a pile of wind-battered deck chairs wrestling in a corner. There were no clubbers now because it was winter and raining and also Monday morning. I could just glimpse the edge of the swimming pool—a bold design choice given that studies had shown significant toxins, including the remnants of chemical weapons, still present in the soil and groundwater. My sense that the club's promoters were embracing their proximity to persistent industrial contamination was based on the flyer for a recent industrial techno night, which showed a tipped-over barrel, clouds of green smoke, and a radioactive warning sign. The slogan on the club's Instagram page read: "A little party never killed nobody!"

Some of the things that made this a good location for a nightclub had also made it a good site for Germany's leading mustard gas factory. Land was cheap. They had few neighbors. No one traveled this way by accident.

The factory was built under the company name: Orgacid Ltd. Siegfried's two bosses from Oranienburg—Dr. Engelhard and Professor Quasebart—were CEO and chairman respectively. They loaded the supervisory board with various contacts from the war ministry and from the Oranienburg laboratory itself.

Orgacid's intentionally vague mission was the "production and distribution of chemical products of all kinds, especially Orgacid," which—since Orgacid itself was a made-up word—was the military-industrial equivalent of a wink. It's remarkable that in creating a shell company to hide their true intentions, they could not think of a less sinister name. Orgacid Ltd. was rubber-stamped in November 1934, and three weeks later they had instructions from the army to begin construction of the factory.

That Siegfried never mentioned the name Orgacid in his memoir or surviving letters was not a big surprise. In the words of historian Olaf Groehler: "Orgacid was a phantom whose existence even its founders could not seem to remember." But given that Orgacid Ltd. was operated by his closest colleagues, using methods he worked with in Oranienburg, I had to think he would have heard about it. He and his family left for Turkey before the factory was fully operational, but I wondered if he ever visited the site and saw his research coming to life, the cooling tower and filling station, the underground channels and storage bunkers. Did he believe that this, too, was no more than being well prepared?

Whatever the answer, Siegfried could not have anticipated that almost eight decades later there would still be residents of Ammendorf whose lives were dedicated to cleaning up the mess.

2.

Erich Gadde—a twinkly-eyed eighty-two-year-old with no email address, a cell phone he doesn't use, one good ear, a many-zipped raincoat, and an accordion briefcase full of evidence documenting a long and varied history of toxicity and industrial malpractice—gave me a tour of his hometown. He was the founder of the Orgacid Citizens' Initiative, a group committed to acknowledging and remediating the legacy of dangerous chemicals in Ammendorf. I had brought my friend Marta, who was simultaneously interpreting the conversation and helping me record it.

We walked alongside the railway tracks, exploring the area on which Erich worked from 1959 until his retirement due to health problems in 1993. It was then that he began noticing the pattern of sickness among those with connections to Orgacid. His brother, Wolfgang, had died of pancreatic cancer at age fifty-seven, after decades of working on the site. His wife and her parents had lived in a house that was tightly wedged between the various workshops and factories. In the photos he showed me, their home looked unfeasible, like it had just fallen out of the sky and landed there among the smokestacks.

His mother-in-law developed a brain tumor and his father-in-law had suffered from both skin cancer and erythrocytosis, a blood disease linked to chemical exposure. Erich had started writing letters to the authorities and making a list of those who had developed similar problems after working or living near the site. That was thirty years ago, and his list now had seventy names on it, including his own. In 2011, he had been diagnosed with pulmonary fibrosis—one of the known long-term complications of exposure to mustard gas.

A woman at the local council described Erich as "the Erin Brockovich of Ammendorf." I admitted to not even knowing that the film was based on a true story. In 1996, Erin Brockovich had helped to successfully sue Pacific Gas & Electric after finding widespread unexplained illness in the town of Hinkley in California. The company was found to have dumped carcinogens in the groundwater. They settled the case for $333 million. But unlike Erin, Erich was not a paralegal with the backing of a law firm and he remained at some distance from an ending suitable for Hollywood. After thirty years of campaigning, the site remained unsafe and he was still battling the profound forces of indifference.

A local journalist told me that Erich called her multiple times a week, always looking for new ways to get the word out. But it was hard to make people care about something they couldn't see. He had assembled a lot of evidence, but was struggling to prove direct causal links between the contamination and human illness. None of the doctors he had approached were willing to go on record saying that Orgacid had made the local population ill. He had campaigned to stop the council from selling the land for commercial use—and failed.

Erich showed us around the businesses that were now using the land. The former administrative office of Orgacid had become rehearsal rooms for bands. The washroom for employees working with toxic materials was now a forecourt for secondhand cars. Rather than expensively decontaminating the site, the local council had simply decided to cover the whole area in two yards of soil, construct an "artificial hill" over the former mustard gas production facilities, then start making money off it. To say that the problem had been swept under the carpet was barely a metaphor. The only caveat for these commercial tenants was: do not dig.

Erich then pointed at the heavy-duty doors of the nightclub and said, "Hopfe. Hopfe. Drug boss." It took a few minutes of googling to realize that this was not a historical reference. The current owner of the land was a spiky-haired forty-five-year-old called Andreas Hopfe, who had rented out the space to the beach bar. For him, this would have been a rational economic decision because these weekend-long parties fitted perfectly with his other concern as a large-scale importer of recreational drugs, thus keeping supply and demand all under one roof. Hopfe was now beginning his more than eight years in prison. In the operation that led to his arrest, the police had hacked his messages and reportedly discovered that the former poison factory was one of the buildings used to process hundreds of kilos of cannabis, cocaine, heroin, and amphetamines. During the subsequent raids, the police seized bags of cash, assault rifles, luxury cars, and a speedboat.

As I started eagerly taking photos of the nightclub, Erich looked on with an air of disappointment. This was half the problem. It was easy enough to get people to pay attention to a lurid story of transnational crime, but much harder to make them care about the underlying issues—a history stretching back almost a century.

German stockpiles of chemical weapons were never deployed during the Second World War. Even as they used hydrogen cyanide for murder on an industrial scale, the Nazis resisted chemical warfare. Hitler himself had a personal aversion to battle gases. He claimed to have been temporarily blinded by a British mustard gas attack while in the trenches in 1918—after which his eyes, he wrote, "turned into glowing coals." His doctor from the time had said Hitler was suffering from hysterical blindness—and suggested that either he was faking it or he had rubbed his eyes until they matched the injuries he was hoping for. It nevertheless became a key part of his personal narrative: from soldier to Führer, blind man to visionary. And two decades later, at the height of war, he ultimately decided against the deployment of poison gases on the front lines. Whether his decision was purely strategic or, at some level, an expression of his personal experience with chemical warfare is difficult to say. Either way it created the uneasy situation in which my great-grandfather's work might have been far more lethal without an intervention from Hitler.

As it was, Ammendorf's enormous stockpiles of chemicals were still in place when first the Americans and then the Russians arrived at the end of the war. In 1945, the Red Army went through the factories, stripping out any worthwhile equipment, and blowing up what they didn't want. Recent documentation shows that local workers were forced to burn 726 metric tons of mustard gas in an improvised incinerator. It goes without saying that this was not a scientifically approved way to dispose of a swimming pool's worth of carcinogens.

After we had been walking for a while, Erich had to stop for a minute to turn away and cough. He had been only three years old when the sky above the town filled with smoke. Then, during the thirty years he had spent working the small length of railway line that ran through the factories, he had often been aware of the sharp smell in his nostrils.

He got his breath back and wanted to keep going.

We walked along the edge of a busy road, then peeled off onto a nondescript stretch of muddy ground about the size of a tennis court. Erich pointed to the ground and explained that only now were we officially trespassing. My boots slipped on the silt and revealed concrete beneath. This had been the filling station where the liquid Lost was poured into shells and bombs by workers who suffered a predictably high rate of sickness. Somewhere beneath the ground, and under the busy road, was the channel along which a river of chemicals had flowed from the nearby factory. Nobody knew the exact location. The original plans, if they still existed, had never been found.

We reached a metal fence that stopped us from exploring any further. The sign said *Risk of death—Do not enter—Parents are responsible for their children.* In 1979, there had been a scandal in West Germany when three young boys found their way into the unsecured remains of a Second World War chemical weapons plant near Hamburg. Locals had long been protesting the presence of the factory in their community, standing behind the slogan: "Lost = Death." The boys had clambered around among ruins that contained hundreds of tons of decaying ammunition, ordnance, poison gases, and eight chemical grenades found rotting in a toilet. One of the boys, eight-year-old Oliver Ludwig, was killed in an explosion and the other two were badly injured.

Erich, Marta, and I all peered through the fence. Until recently, this land had been left open, densely overgrown, home to a few fly-tipped televisions and torn bags of rubbish. That all changed last year when a local councillor, Johannes Streckenbach, stumbled across a surprise while exploring the site with a scientist: a deep hole in the ground and freshly dug. There was a ladder sticking out and a pair of boots nearby. It seemed the councillor had interrupted someone. The hole was a yard wide and two yards deep, and there was a smell so abrasive that Councillor Streckenbach could not stand there—and soon his head was pounding. When he reported this find to the waste management company that owns the site, they could not explain it. They came the next day to examine the hole, but found it filled in. And that's when they put up the fence.

3.

I arranged to meet Erich and Marta back at the council office, then I continued to walk along the perimeter. I wanted a closer look at the hole.

In a pause in the traffic, I scrambled through a bush and out of sight of the busy road. The fence turned a corner and ran along the edge of an open field dominated by two giant electricity pylons. At the far end, I saw a line of five deer skirt a wall before bounding away into the no-go area. Here was the accidental rewilding that comes with profound industrial contamination. I followed the deer. Where the fence met a brick wall, there was a V-shaped gap, perfect for animals and those who do not suffer from persistent back pain. I chucked my backpack over—perhaps I had seen that in films—then very slowly squeezed through.

I wondered if this was a place where fumes still lingered from a poison made according to my great-grandfather's instructions. How much of his research had ended up in the soil in places like this—beyond the reach of the Geneva Convention?

As I traced the deer tracks, the bushes soon closed in and I was plucking barbs from my clothes and hair. The satellite view on my phone showed the location of the hole, probably no more than fifty yards away, but I couldn't find a way through. Eventually I went on all fours and then onto my belly and, by the time I found the hole, I was sweating and breathing hard. I didn't ask myself *why* I wanted to experience Siegfried's work, firsthand. Was it a perverse kind of intimacy? A taste of the family recipe?

The hole had been covered with a tarpaulin, its edges staked out. The entire area was primitively camouflaged beneath a big pile of branches. Beside the tarpaulin lay the rusted head of a pickax. When I tried to pull out one of the stakes it came away easily, the earth crumbly and white. Peeling back the edges of the tarp, I knelt down and peered inside. There was the sharp smell. When I stood up I felt woozy and had to reach out for balance. I allowed myself to believe that this was it, that Lost was reaching me across the decades—that it had nothing to do with the twenty minutes I had just spent scrabbling through brambles in a padded coat. I thought of how Siegfried had always feared that one day his poisons might leak out and hurt his family. What he could not have known was that his family would come looking for them.

4.

Entering the council office felt like walking into a war room. Laid out on the long conference table were maps, architectural plans, sets of aerial photographs showing the Orgacid site before and after its destruction by the Russians, documents from archives in Moscow, Washington, and London, out-of-print books on the history of German chemical weapons, and standing all around the table—deep in conversation—were Councillor Streckenbach, Erich Gadde, local historian Wolfram Fischer, and Professor Johannes Preuss, an expert on chemical weapons in Germany.

Listening to the urgency with which they discussed the latest developments, it did not feel like history. They picked apart the results of a recent study into local contaminants, previously unseen floor plans received from a Soviet archive in Moscow, a new source claiming that forced laborers had been killed in a 1942 factory fire, Erich's forthcoming publication of his research, not to mention an ever-growing list of theories about who had dug the mysterious hole in the ground.

Perhaps the trespassers had been searching for scrap metal? But then—why seek out a particularly toxic part of the site? Were they detectorists? Or were they ex-employees, like Erich, with specific knowledge of the history and layout of Orgacid? Were they seeking access to a shaft that would lead to the sewer running beneath the site? What else was down there? When I suggested my own theory that the hole had been dug by the local drug boss—because what better place to bury a suitcase full of money than in a forgotten chemical weapons bunker—Councillor Streckenbach calmly offered me three fact-based reasons why he was "very sure that Mr. Hopfe has nothing to do with it." Even so, the hole was a useful puzzle, a way to keep Orgacid in the local, if not national, news. A recent headline read: "What Lies Hidden on the Site of the Former Nazi Poison Factory?" The drone-assisted photo showed the rubble bleached white by chemicals, a ladder disappearing into darkness.

In my backpack, I had pages 1,692 to 1,694 of Siegfried's memoir, the part of his confession where he expressed his shame and regret at having worked with chemical weapons. Since none of the people affected by the contaminants in Ammendorf had ever received any form of acknowledgment or apology, let alone compensation, despite decades of campaigning, I wondered if Siegfried's remorse might mean something to Erich Gadde.

I handed over the pages and watched him read. It was a long five minutes in which I did not know what to do with my hands. A part of me had imagined that I might see the ripples on his glass of water as, his hand shaking with emotion, he tried to lift the drink to his lips. But I could already tell by the slight impatience with which he was reading, his head very subtly shaking from side to side, that this was not going to be one of those moments.

He put down the sheets of paper and said, "I can't . . . This isn't . . ." He shook his head. "I really can't say anything about that." It took a few moments to recognize what was going on. He looked down at the pages and said: "On behalf of all Germans, I apologize." I should have understood that Erich would not accept remorse from a Jewish chemist. But equally it felt absurd that he should apologize to me and so I apologized to him for putting him in a position where he felt he needed to apologize, the two of us boxed in on all sides by regrets. In the silence that followed I realized that there was no way for us to speak across these tangled pasts, one history making it impossible to acknowledge the other.

We were both relieved, then, to dive back into the blissful release of the documents on the table: the maps, photos, plans, and toxicology reports. We shared our research with each other— swapping photocopies and books bristling with Post-it notes—in lieu of complicated feelings. As we worked, I thought about my great-grandfather spending fourteen years on a memoir in which he never actually said what he needed to. I could hear the steady clatter of Siegfried's typewriter in the sound of Councillor Streckenbach, in the next room, sending an email.

5.

Erich and I stood in the doorway of a derelict electrochemical plant, sheltering from the rain. After five hours in each other's company discussing industrial toxins, conversation had finally come round to an utterly meaningless subject about which we could both express strong feelings. He told me he supported the local soccer team, Halle, in the third German league.

"Are they good?" I asked.

"*Nein,*" he said, smiling. "*Nicht gut.*"

The rain was easing. All around us the buildings had been demolished or become picturesque ruins, creepers climbing in through smashed windows.

"*Und Swansea?*" he asked. "*Ist Swansea gut?*"

"*Nein,*" I said. "*Nicht gut.*"

The last thing we did together was stand on the pavement, breathing the foul smell from a line of semis queuing to join the bypass road. This was the spot where he hoped there would soon be a noticeboard acknowledging the complex history of this place that—he believed, but could not definitively prove—had taken the

life of his brother and many others. Erich and Councillor Streckenbach had been working together on the text, which described the
26,000 tons of poisons manufactured here, more than a third of
all the chemical weapons produced by Germany during the Second
World War. The text ended with a reminder that the "facilities and
sewers, all the way to the White Elster river, are still in place."

Erich was confident that, eventually, they would get the sign
installed. After all it was probably the council's cheapest conceivable
concession to a problem they would prefer to forget. There had been
talk about turning the area into a "climate-neutral industrial park,"
a wonderful idea in which Erich had precisely no hope. For now,
though, there were still some issues about the sign's exact location,
since local businesses tended to resist being publicly linked to the
Nazi war machine. We looked out at the tops of the freight containers
in a nearby self-storage facility. Opposite us, family vehicles shone
in the wet on the forecourt of Micha's secondhand cars.

6.

Three months later, Councillor Streckenbach emailed me the results of the preliminary soil analysis from the "mysterious hole"—the illegal excavation both he and I had visited. With characteristic dynamism, the City of Halle had commissioned this study in order to answer the question: Should we commission more studies? The answer was yes. Of the substances with potential to contaminate the groundwater, lead was detected at a concentration nine hundred times higher than the limit required to trigger further research. Chromium was found at thirty-four times that limit, though the report did not give details of which specific compound. (In the groundwater in Hinkley, Erin Brockovich had found chromium-6, which is mutagenic, carcinogenic, and causes severe respiratory damage.) The laboratory also noted a dangerous concentration of barium, a toxic industrial metal with causal links to, among other health risks, chronic breathing problems like those of Erich Gadde. The list went on, taking in a variety of industrial by-products and even thorium, the radioactive element in Siegfried's toothpaste. What the laboratory did *not* find, however, were any decomposition chemicals from mustard gas. I had achieved no contact with Siegfried across the decades, and I had, in fact, only succeeded in revealing the extent to which he and I shared delusions of grandeur. My visit to the hole had exposed me to a whole rainbow of toxins, but they weren't the right ones.

The results of the study legally obliged the City of Halle to take action, but did not specify the speed at which they had to do so. I heard that Erich, now eighty-three, was spending his own money to pay for blood tests that might finally, undeniably prove a link between the toxins in the ground and those in the bodies of Ammendorf's residents. It was a long shot because those toxins would likely have been metabolized by now, decades after exposure—but he still wanted to try. His most pressing concern was that the problems in Ammendorf would be resolved, not from any remediation of the land, but by his own death, after which the city would just quietly move on. And all the while he was adding new names to his list of the sick.

He had also published his research at last: an article titled "Death Came from Ammendorf," the culmination of decades of work. The essay was a compact but complete history of the site, its contaminants, its victims, and ongoing governmental failures. That his exposé had not been picked up by local or national press was perhaps partly due to it being buried on page 300 of an academic journal from the German Chemistry Museum in Merseburg. Meanwhile, on Instagram, the nightclub was advertising its summer season of pool parties: shots, bombs, and sangria buckets; free entry and a flower necklace for the first hundred through the door.

7.

Back in Berlin, I called my mother and told her all about the trip that she was glad to have missed. I admitted that I had no plans to visit any of the other former chemical weapons factories with links to Auer, of which there were many. The truth was that having spent two years reading about poison gases, learning more than I could want to know about secondary infections in mustard gas blisters, I was looking forward to a change.

In his memoir, Siegfried described his own sense of relief at finally leaving behind his work with chemical weapons when he and his family moved to Turkey: "a heavy burden was lifted from me because I was now free of this hated task. . . . I did not mention a single word to the Turks about my knowledge in the field of warfare agents, although I would certainly have strengthened my position by doing so."

He started working for the Turkish Red Crescent, a long-standing charitable organization equivalent to the International Red Cross. This was a job he could be proud of and it became one of the well-known details among my family. I liked how it gave balance to his life story, from lethal gases to humanitarian aid. It was comforting to think that just four months after coauthoring an article with a paid-up Nazi, he was starting a different life on the elevated plains of Anatolia. So although their emigration had been far more comfortable and not nearly as heroic as I first imagined it—no heist on their home, no dash to the border—I was still excited to write about Siegfried's fresh start.

The Jewish Museum in Berlin had dozens of letters from Siegfried and Lilli to the family members they were leaving behind in Germany. My mother agreed to help with the translations and slowly we built up a picture of their journey east, starting with the lapis-blue carriages of the *Orient Express* waiting on the platform in Munich. The restaurant car had white tablecloths and white-jacketed waiters, who brought dishes from whichever of the ten countries they happened to be passing through at the time. The Merzbachers ate and slept their way through Salzburg, Linz, Vienna, Bratislava, Budapest, and Belgrade, the conductor letting them know when to wind on their watches. At each border, the train was hitched to a new, local engine, so that the journey resembled a relay race, a baton passed across the continent. Through the window they watched the muddy Danube widen.

The final stop was at Sirkeci in Istanbul, a station built right down by the water, the far edge of the continent. It was here that Siegfried deposited Lilli and the children before traveling on alone to make arrangements for their new life. He took the ferry from Europe to Asia and then caught the *Anadolu Ekspres* eastward, an overnight train that puttered gently alongside the Marmara Sea, past the fishing villages on its shores. He slept beautifully and woke to find himself passing through a startling and seemingly endless landscape, the beautiful emptiness and space of central Anatolia—sand, stone, brush, the low hills dotted with huts, sheep, and goats. And then he saw it in the distance: Ankara, the pristine capital of the young republic.

He stepped out from the station into Yenişehir—*New Town*. Everywhere he walked were wide streets, freshly landscaped parks, and the smell of wet cement. He stood beneath a giant bronze of two topless men, one representing the old ways—bearded, bald, reaching out for balance—and the other the new—young, ripped, and pointing his rifle to the sky. Although Ankara had been a significant settlement for thousands of years, it was now a city determined to discard its history and start again.

Over the following weeks, Siegfried was introduced to a ready-made community of German Jews. Since 1933, the Turkish government had actively offered jobs to select intellectuals exiled from Germany. By 1935, hundreds of the world's leading musicians, architects, surgeons, anthropologists, botanists, conductors, and physicists were living in Istanbul and Ankara, helping to establish modern universities, hospitals, and orchestras. Once the family was settled in, my grandmother took violin lessons with Gilbert Back—formerly a leading member of the Berlin Philharmonic. When Siegfried broke his arm, the bone was set by one famous surgeon, then massaged daily by another. My grandmother's brother went to study physics for four years at Istanbul University in a department where German-Jewish Nobel laureates dropped in to give guest lectures.

One of the jokes from the time was:

Where's the best German university?

Istanbul.

And for a long time, that's all I imagined when I thought about the fourteen years the Merzbachers spent in Ankara—essentially the Bloomsbury group, but with better weather. I had also seen pictures of the broad-shouldered headquarters of the Turkish Red Crescent with its manicured gardens and a kiosk where the public could buy health-giving mineral water. This seemed like the kind of place where burdens are lifted. But that was before I had read his work correspondence.

8.

I brought the pile of paper to my parents' house in Wales, copies of sixty-one typewritten letters from the Berlin Jewish Museum. Long after our family's emigration, Siegfried and his old German boss, Professor Quasebart, had remained in regular written contact. My mother sighed when I handed them over.

Despite eighteen months of classes at the Goethe-Institut, I was still nowhere near my stated goal of understanding the language of advanced German chemistry, an ambition at which my tutor had laughed long and hard. Over the next few weeks, my mother sent me her handwritten translations in the post. Scientific paragraphs were sometimes rendered as *technical blah blah* and she left comments in the margins—*dead right!* or *really?!!*—and on occasion she'd phone with a live update, saying that Siegfried's tone was now "all crawl and creep." I was particularly struck that he signed off one of his letters to Quasebart with "I am your very devoted servant"—though my mother told me that this was, for the time, a "fairly common form of grovelling." In her complex system of highlighter pens, each theme was lit up in a different color: red for chemical weapons, yellow for poor health, green for the Nazis. With just a casual flick through the pages, I could see that the Ankara letters contained a lot more red and green than expected.

In this way I learned that Siegfried's job at the Turkish Red Crescent was in no way equivalent to being a doctor for Médicins Sans Frontières. Half his wages were still being paid by Auer in Berlin. In fact, his old company had covered the full cost of his family's emigration; they paid for that Bechstein grand piano to be shipped a thousand miles east. He and his family were fleeing the Nazis while remaining reliant on them, a contradiction which would only become more problematic in the years that followed.

As I read the translated letters, I had to wonder why Siegfried had saved so much of this correspondence. Perhaps he had always planned to write about it one day. After all, the seventh volume of his memoir did start with a promise to describe his "new tasks at the Turkish Red Crescent in Ankara"—before he got distracted with 150 pages of summarizing his encyclopedia.

Again I asked my mother if she wanted to join me on a research trip, this time to Ankara. She liked the idea, but some friends of hers were already planning a walking holiday then. They were going to hike the Lycian Way in Anatolia—a historic coastal path, with pine trees and blue seas—and she'd probably do that instead.

IV.
Young Republic

1.

Siegfried was naked at the sink in his Ankara hotel room, washing away the memory of his long journey, when he heard a knock at the door. Standing in the corridor in his suit and striped tie, looking rested, was Professor Quasebart. Siegfried's past had arrived in Ankara ahead of him.

Siegfried was asked to "please stay entirely in the background" while Quasebart and some men from Oranienburg took care of negotiations about his new role. Apparently there were still some doubts about Siegfried. He heard rumors that he was, depending on who you spoke to, too quiet, too old, too German, or too Jewish. Each morning, Siegfried stayed in his room, listening to the clomping feet of his former colleagues as they went out at dawn to consider his attributes. He wrote furious letters to Lilli in Istanbul about how the whole situation "makes your blood boil in your veins." After three anxious days, he was finally deemed trustworthy and appointed codirector at a new gas mask factory, a joint venture between the Turkish Red Crescent and Auer. At the grand opening, Professor Quasebart gave the Turkish prime minister, Ismet Inönü, a tour of the premises.

The gas mask "is today no longer a weapon of the army but a tool of every house and business," the prime minister said, in a speech where he was flanked by hard-jawed men in uniform.

I walked through the gardens of Ankara's museum of military history, passing rows of enormous, German-made machines that loomed like the exhibits in a dinosaur park—contraptions for pressurizing ammunition, shaping howitzer barrels, and deep-hole drilling. At the gate, an armed guard scanned my belongings, then took possession of my passport because nothing is more welcoming to a researcher than locking away their travel documents. Once inside, I soon found an ostrich-shaped machine for testing the elasticity of the rubber in gas masks. The label read: *Auer, Berlin*.

I knew that Turkey and Germany had a close relationship. In 1935, Siegfried had arrived in Istanbul at a German-designed train station, crossed a German-made bridge as he traveled on to Ankara, a capital laid out by two German city planners. By 1936, more than half of Turkey's exports were sold to Germany. And while Turkey remained neutral for most of the war, in practice they continued to supply most of the chromium the German military needed for its guns, planes, and ammunition. Deutsche Bank, meanwhile, sold in Istanbul hundreds of pounds of precious metals stolen from Holocaust victims, including wedding rings and dental gold. Not that any of this context was on display in the museum of military history.

As seemed to be the pattern with these kinds of places, it was fantastically well funded with no one inside. I strolled through a history of Turkish weaponry, all the way from Ottoman scimitars up to the very latest in naval cannons that could fire eighty long-distance shells a minute. I found a display case containing one of Siegfried's gas masks, produced under his direction between 1937 and 1938. It was chunky and gray, a hose like an elephant's trunk running to the boxy filter. On its side was the symbol of the Turkish Red Crescent and nearby were more photos of the organization's imposing headquarters. But this was not where Siegfried worked. The gas mask factory and its associated industries were tucked away just outside the city. An old black-and-white photo showed a scattering of structures on a bare hill. One could mistake them for farm buildings except for an unusually prominent chimney.

Afterward, I walked through the busy shopping streets of Kızılay, googling as I went. The headquarters of the Turkish Red Crescent had long ago been demolished and, of the three apartments in which my family used to live, none still existed. For two out of the three, the whole street was gone. There was no sign of the Bauhaus-inspired exterior of the first apartment or the apricot orchard they could see from their balcony in the third. I started to wonder if this trip was likely to be anything more than an act of imagination. The metropolis I was walking through had no horizons, sprawled in all directions, and was home to nearly 6 million. Somewhere far beneath it was Siegfried's Ankara, a small city of open skies, where the new roads were laid with asphalt while the side streets were still earth. Atatürk Boulevard was built as the city's central spine, its wide, tree-lined borders intended as an idealized Parisian thoroughfare. The trees were now gone, and it was clogged with four lanes of traffic which gave it an air of actual Paris.

For all the change in Ankara, there was still one highly visible connection to its early days. The face of Kemal Pasha Atatürk, the founder of modern Turkey, popped up everywhere on statues, posters, and paintings, the great tectonic wrinkles of his forehead as recognizable as the flag itself. I passed a primary school along the entire length of which was a stylized mural of the War of Independence—the battle from which Atatürk emerged as a military and political leader. At the end of the First World War, the Ottoman Empire had collapsed and was partitioned and occupied by Allied forces. The painting showed Atatürk leading the fight back: his men riding horses, swinging swords, and firing cannons while, behind them in the bay, Greek and French gunships were tipped up and sinking. Between 1919 and 1923, his forces pushed the Allies out and eventually established the boundaries of a new state, the Republic of Turkey. Moving the capital to Ankara, he set about building a secular nation that would be thoroughly modern in every way, including an up-to-date military.

I took the metro to the eastern suburb of Mamak. In the photo I'd found at the museum, the gas mask factory and its surrounding buildings were the only thing out here, which presumably explained why the original street address had been just Gas Mask Factory, Mamak. Except Mamak was now one of Ankara's sprawling commuter suburbs, where a raised trainline threaded between rows of high-rises. I felt faintly ridiculous while consulting my black-and-white photo of a mostly bare landscape through which Siegfried would have traveled each day, bouncing around on the rough roads until the car tilted uphill, its wheels meeting the well-kept private track to the factory.

His letters revealed that his work in Turkey was not humanitarian. Although there were plans to eventually make gas masks for the civilian population, the first priority was the military. By 1937 they had supplied twenty thousand masks to the Turkish army. And just as in Oranienburg, the Mamak gas mask factory operated an open-door policy between defense and attack, located as it was "next to the poison gas laboratory." In 1943, any pretense at loftier aims was abandoned as the factory was taken over by the Ministry of Defense. Siegfried's bosses were now two colonels and his role was "purely military." As he hinted to an old colleague in Oranienburg, "Of course for a long time now its not only gas masks that are being manufactured."

I walked in what I hoped was the right direction, doubting myself as I passed phone shops, barbers, and a bubblegum-pink café selling pistachio éclairs. But as I started up the hill, I noticed a double-fronted store stocking military uniforms and then a hole-in-the-wall gun shop outside of which stood a mannequin in full camo, deep pockmarks in its polystyrene head.

Siegfried's codirector at the gas mask factory was a Turkish chemist called Dr. Nuri Refet, whom he described as a "loyal friend." Refet was younger than Siegfried, handsome and worldly, a German-speaking, German-educated chemical weapons expert who had regularly published articles in *Die Gasmaske*. When President Atatürk's house had an infestation of red ants in 1937, it was Dr. Refet who dealt with the problem using hydrogen cyanide, the pesticide Zyklon B. He was also the author of numerous Turkish books on chemical weapons, including educational texts like *Combat Gases for Secondary Schools*. I couldn't find any of his work in the city's bookshops, but there was one listed online. A friend of mine in Ankara agreed to receive the package at his office and regretted it when his colleagues saw him holding the slightly moldy copy of

War Gases from 1937. It was published at a time when Dr. Refet and Siegfried were codirectors—and, when I opened it in my hotel room, a yellowing letter came tumbling out, just as it would have done in a film. And just like in a film, I unfolded the letter and discovered it was an actual military document acknowledging the receipt of German-made equipment with which to train Turkish troops in the use of mustard gas. I imagined all my future research would be that easy and, to an extent, I was right.

At the top of the hill, the former gas mask factory was simple to locate on account of it still being a gas mask factory. I stopped outside a security kiosk beneath a big yellow sign that read *Makine ve Kimya Endüstrisi (MKE)*—Machinery and Chemical Industry. In case the name was too subtle, the company had also erected a large outdoor video screen to showcase their latest products. Standing on the pavement, I watched gun turrets swivel and blast tracer fire into the night; uniformed men applauding as distant objects burst into flames; a gunship launching into the sea; fist-sized artillery barrels pointing down the lens of the camera; and a man with a grenade launcher, his expression hidden behind the insectoid eyes of the latest full-face gas mask. These products were spliced together with the kind of fast editing you get in a sports montage.

As I watched the screen, I realized that I was, in turn, being watched by an armed guard, standing nearby with a semiautomatic across his chest. A man with a gun guarding a video of men with guns. A sign said: *NO PHOTOS*. Was it Epicurus, the ancient philosopher, who wrote that a man who causes fear cannot be free from fear? I would have to wait until the evening to check that quote because I was too scared to reach into my pocket.

As the video made clear, MKE was the state's leading manufacturer of military hardware, producing everything from air-portable howitzers to the whole "family of light arms ammunition." They were proud of their long history in Mamak, having emerged from, among other things, the gas mask factory of 1935. Nowadays, the company's most successful product was the new standard rifle for the Turkish infantry, designed for all-weather and high-altitude combat, and the first of its kind that was "100% local and national."

I recognized that phrase. In Siegfried's letters, he regularly mentioned his Turkish bosses' concern that the gas masks should be free of foreign imports—while still meeting German standards. His German bosses, meanwhile, wanted to keep making money from exporting materials to Turkey without giving away their proprietary research. Siegfried was stuck in the middle, navigating two sets of employers, each with their own similar but incompatible nationalist politics.

Lilli saw the problem with more clarity than her husband. "We have to do whatever it takes to become independent of other people as quickly as possible," she wrote, suggesting that they "get away quickly from the old company. In these matters, we are still too naïve." Naivety was a generous word for it.

Siegfried conducted gas mask tests with nitrochloroform, phosgene, tear gas, and hydrogen cyanide, then shared the results of these tests with Professor Quasebart in Berlin. This knowledge exchange went both ways: his Turkish colleagues regularly visited Oranienburg to be updated on the latest poison gas technologies, while his German colleagues came out to Ankara to help with production and training. At times, Mamak started to seem like an outer suburb of Berlin.

In April 1937, Siegfried wrote a confidential letter to Professor

Quasebart. The information was so sensitive that he did not even trust it to Auer's mail room, and so he had it delivered by hand. He explained that his Turkish colleagues wanted to "order larger quantities of the chemicals the department that used to be under my leadership works with," which was his slightly euphemistic way of asking to buy significant amounts of chemical weapons. Siegfried wrote that Dr. Refet, his codirector, would "be traveling to Germany alongside some other gentlemen (all paid for by the Turkish government), for which the question I have previously touched on seems to be a key motivator."

What surprised me was the extent to which I was still capable of finding this a surprise. At some level I clearly could not let go of the belief that Siegfried's memoir was fundamentally trustworthy and that he had nothing to hide. I felt this way partly because I knew he had kept all these letters. Most people involved with this work had made every effort to destroy the documentation. It would have been far easier to bin these papers or let them rot away in a basement rather than carry them round for decades. Why simultaneously deny all involvement and preserve evidence to the contrary? Was it possible he simply hadn't seen any of this as a problem? He had just been putting colleagues in touch with colleagues. Nothing more than a simple moment of networking.

2.

Back at the hotel, I called my mother.

"How are you?" she said. "*Where* are you?"

She had given me the three addresses of our old family apartments in Ankara and I explained that none of them still existed. In fact all that remained of our shared history in modern-day Ankara was the enormous military-industrial complex on the hill.

She made a slow groaning noise.

After reading my mother's translation of the April 1937 letter, I had speculatively typed, *Turkish government German chemical weapons 1937* into Google and the results of that search were what convinced me I needed to visit Mamak in person. Turkish historians had recently uncovered documents that showed that—four months after Siegfried's letter to Quasebart—the Turkish government did approve the purchase of chemical weapons from Germany. They then used them as part of a campaign of brutal killings against ethnic minority groups in Dersim, a mountainous region in the east of Turkey. I had spoken to various experts on this history, including Taner Akçam, a smiley and good-natured professor of genocide studies at UCLA, who told me that Siegfried's letter could be "the breakthrough that fills the vacuum." Another academic, this one based in Istanbul, would not speak on record, but warned me that this area of research was the single most sensitive subject in modern Turkish history, a topic that, in official narratives, remains completely . . .

"Obliterated?" my mother suggested.

"Obliterated."

"Well, I'm not surprised," she said. "You might have to be a bit— to be very careful. You don't need to be a journalist about it."

This was her way of reminding me that I wasn't one. She wished me luck with traveling five hundred miles farther east to a place that, officially, did not exist.

3.

The road carved through the hillside. I watched the taxi driver swerve out wide to navigate fallen rocks. It was mid-February and we were driving through the steep valleys of the Munzur Mountains, headed for Dersim, a small hill town whose name cannot be found on any maps, in textbooks or tourist guides. In the car with me was my friend Eleanor who was going to help me record the interviews. The taxi driver stopped at the first of many military checkpoints and chatted cheerfully to a smiling young woman across whose chest hung an enormous gun. He told her we were on our way to Tunceli.

It had been nearly ninety years since the government changed the town's name, just one of the policies intended to bring this region in line with modern Turkey. Local Armenian, Kurdish, and Zazaki place-names were erased and replaced with Turkish ones. Even the words "Kurd," "Kurdish," and "Kurdistan" were forbidden in government language, so that the people living in these hills were known only as "mountain Turks." This area was self-reliant, self-governing, religious, and non-Turkish speaking, all things deemed incompatible with the new state. An internal report from 1926 described Dersim as "a dangerous abscess . . . that must be operated on decisively."

As we continued through the valley, we could see on the peaks of the mountains above us a sequence of watchtowers, panopticons that loomed over the landscape. The driver explained there were more than twenty of them peering down. We entered a tunnel through a cliff and soon emerged in the next valley, where it was snowing, big slushy clumps that made the windshield wipers judder. For the government, the challenge of controlling this region had been partly geographical, the steep mountains protecting the communities within them. Through the 1930s, roads were laid and tunnels drilled—making the kind of infrastructure you could drive a truck down. By the spring of 1937, around 25,000 troops had been sent to the region and Prime Minister Inönü said that these "precipitous valleys and inaccessible mountains" would soon feel "just as though they were the streets of Ankara."

We stopped at another checkpoint, showed our passports, then drove up a steep switchback road into what was either Dersim or Tunceli, depending on who you spoke to. As we drove to our hotel, we passed the enormous police barracks in the center of town, high-walled and razor-wired, then navigated around the numerous police officers walking in the streets and standing beside squad cars with their blue lights flashing, all of which made me think that they must be responding to an incident. It was only after a few days in Dersim that I understood this was a town in a state of high alert that stretched far back into the previous century. In Turkish, Tunceli means "bronze fist."

In the American-style diner of our hotel, we met our local guide to the area's history. Metin Albaslan was thirty-seven, lightly bearded, shaggy haired, and with a pronounced V-shaped hairline that gave him the air of a very relaxed vampire. He and I had been chatting for weeks on WhatsApp, during which time I had tried to reconcile his extensive use of silly emoji with a photo I'd seen online: across his back was an enormous tattoo of an AK-47. He spent two years in prison for his association with the banned Kurdistan Workers' Party (PKK), that, since the 1970s, has been engaged in violent battles for Kurdish autonomy in the east, and are considered a terrorist organization by Turkey, the European Union, and the United States. I had read an interview in which Metin explained that the tattoo was inspired not by an actual gun but by the dramatic ridged peak above Dersim, which is shaped like a Kalashnikov, a detail that I found reassuring. Now that we had a clear view of the ridge itself, I struggled to see the resemblance.

After lunch, we were joined by our interpreter, who I'm calling Kerem, a young Kurdish academic with perfect English, left-wing politics, and a deep love of Virginia Woolf. He smoked whenever possible and asked that we not use his real name. A 2016 law meant that academics were forbidden from speaking to the press without government approval and since then six thousand academics had lost their jobs for holding the wrong opinions.

Metin took us to the battered Tata pickup he'd borrowed from a friend and we all piled in. He drove us down the hill—stopping at another checkpoint—and then on into a steep-sided valley. Metin had been worried that the roads would be blocked by snow, but most of it had already melted. This was fortunate because ours was not a vehicle you would want to rely on. The air vents weren't working so we had to take turns wiping condensation from inside the windshield using Metin's red beanie hat. There was a typo printed over the truck's wheel arches: *Of Road.*

After half an hour in the car I was gripping the seat beneath me. In the lead-up to the trip, my sciatica had flared up so that now, whenever possible, I jumped out of the vehicle to pace back and forth like a zoo animal. My jacket pockets rattled with packs of naproxen and Tylenol 3. Eleanor had wondered if there might be a connection between my physical discomfort and the uncomfortable subjects I was going to talk about. I was of the opinion that my nerve pain was just bad timing, nothing more. When we stopped at the next checkpoint, I swallowed a fistful of pills.

Before coming to Dersim, I had made sure that Metin and Kerem—and everyone we hoped to talk to—were aware of my family history. I had no intention of surprising anyone with the news that I was the descendant of someone who may have facilitated a local massacre. Above all I wanted to give them the opportunity to tell me to not come at all. A part of me was even hoping they would say that. Instead I experienced nothing but kindness and hospitality and that was, in its way, harder to accept.

We pulled over in a rest area with an incredible view. Beneath us, the Munzur River curved sharply away into a steep canyon, coiling between enormous boulders. For the Alevi people of this region, this was their holy river, flowing with water that can make wishes come true. Rising from the water were the cliffs of Halvori, known locally as the '38 Rocks. This was where Seyid Riza, one of Dersim's most respected political and religious leaders, had sworn on the river that he would resist military control, and this was also where that resistance was broken. After Riza had been executed without meaningful trial, the army rounded up local people, civilians, and murdered them here, in part to defile the river's spiritual significance. Men were tied together in the hundreds and shot with machine guns. Women and children were killed with bayonets to save on ammunition. Bodies were burned or dumped in the river so that, in the words of a survivor who was a child at the time, "the water flowed bloody." An estimated 420 men, women, and children were murdered by the army in two days.

"Every rock, every mountaintop, every corner of this river contains such stories," Metin said, and we listened to the water rushing far beneath us until the sound was drowned out by a Chinook helicopter passing low overhead. Metin did not glance up. According to official data released by the Turkish government, 13,160 Dersimi civilians were murdered across 1937 and 1938. Other historians suggest the death toll was four times this number but, since only one government-approved historian has ever been given full access to the archives, the debate remains intentionally one-sided. Legal campaigns to have mass grave sites officially recognized are mired in bureaucracy. There are no information boards or permanent memorials in Dersim—only the military watchtowers that look down from the hills. Even in the town's well-funded public museum, with its detailed history of the region, there was not one mention of the massacres—unless you count the fact that the building itself was originally built as an army barracks in 1937.

We got back in the truck and continued driving down into the valley. Eventually Metin parked up by the river, the cliffs rising steeply all around us, a line of bare birch trees along the bank. He pointed across the water to where a slit of light shone from a sheer ravine, a gap barely wide enough for one person to clamber through. This was the entry point to the Laç valley, the last refuge for the Kurdish Alevis fleeing the massacres. They chose this valley specifically for its inaccessibility, hiking far into the mountains and hiding in caves they hoped the army could not reach.

The four of us huddled at the side of the road. The fading light had turned everything black-and-white and I was increasingly aware of the occasional headlights that swept across us. I saw Eleanor move to hide her microphone beneath her scarf, though her enormous headphones were a giveaway.

The Turkish army used chemical weapons in the Laç valley caves. The state had always denied it, but in 1986 an aging Turkish politician let something slip in an interview. "They used poison gas," he said. "They poisoned them like rats from inside the entrance to the caves." Since then, military documents have slowly started to emerge. In 2008, a document was uncovered that showed President Atatürk and Prime Minister İnönü jointly signing off on the purchase "by secret negotiation" of twenty tons of German tear and mustard gas in 1937. The following year, they bought planes from America and from the Heinkel factory in Oranienburg. The caves they couldn't reach from the ground were attacked from the air. No one survived. Human bones are still scattered on the cave floors, adults and children, unburied and unnamed. Though these revelations made headlines in Istanbul's left-leaning newspapers— "Turkey Bought Poison Gas from Nazi Germany to Kill Kurdish Alevis and Armenians in 1938"—the news did not trouble the mainstream press. What was missing, in terms of documentation, was corroboration from whichever German company made the sale—documents like the one my great-grandfather wrote to Professor Quasebart.

While we peered into the narrow valley, Metin described the time he'd been up to the caves, a full day's hike from here. He saw the bones for himself. Listening to him talk, I had the sensation that someone was standing inches behind me, staring into the back of my head. I could feel the proximity of feelings that were beyond my capability to feel. This was not helped by the paranoia that every pair of passing headlights must be those of the military coming to interrogate us—until, at last, they were.

A large armored truck trundled past, then stopped a few yards down the road. Its high beams lit up the cliffs. The vehicle itself was so nonreflective as to be almost invisible, a highly aggressive nothingness. On its roof, a radar jammer rotated at the speed of a turntable. Kerem quietly told us to hide our recording equipment as the soldier wound down his window.

"What are you doing out here?" he called.

Metin crossed the road to speak to him, standing beneath the door as they talked. We had been told that if a soldier in the mountains found out what we were discussing, the news would reach the capital the same day. The sensitivities surrounding the use of Nazi poison gas in Dersim were not hard to understand. There was the implicit connection to the Holocaust, and the obvious parallels. This has led to rumors that the Nazis saw Dersim as a proof of concept. There was also the fact that President Atatürk's adopted daughter, Sabiha Gökçen, was one of the pilots in 1938, a mission about which she later said: "I can't forget the excitement of the first bombardment." Then there was the issue that the brutality and oppression of that period continues to this day.

Metin told the soldier: "We are walking and showing our friends nature."

The soldier looked at us, and then he looked up and down the road: the river, the trees, the slit of pale light glowing through the ravine, the snow on the high cliffs.

"What nature?" he said.

Metin's laughter echoed through the valley.

4.

By the time we drove back, the watchtowers had switched on their floodlights so that they glowed in the mist on the hilltops.

"Like spaceships," I said.

"Like the Eye of Sauron," Metin said.

When we reached the checkpoint outside Dersim town, it was well-lit and busy, soldiers leaning into the wound-down windows of stopped cars and vans. They were not letting anyone drive on the Erzincan road, though we didn't know why.

In our hotel room, Metin pulled up a video on his phone. While we'd been by the river, there had been an accident at an American-owned gold mine, a few miles to the northwest. The video showed an enormous mountain of cyanide-laced soil, a by-product of the mining process, as it suddenly gave way and flowed through the valley like water from a burst dam. Rescue teams were now searching for nine missing miners, while the soil continued to slide toward the Euphrates. Environmental activists had tried to shut the mine down because of a previous cyanide leak, but the company simply paid a fine and carried on digging. Not that Metin found any of this surprising, and he put his phone back in his pocket. What had started with the erasing of names became the building of tunnels and barracks, the forced resettlements, the massacres, the burning of homes and farmland, the poison gas, the watchtowers, the checkpoints, and now the landscape itself, flooded for dams or sold off for gold mines. By the evening, protesters in Istanbul were marching beneath the placard: *Not an accident but a massacre.*

5.

Metin wanted us to meet Ali Ekber Kaya, the former president of the local Human Rights Association, and someone who had dedicated his life to documenting events in Dersim. As we walked through town, it was raining so hard that the pavement seemed to boil and streams ran down through the streets. In the valley below, the Munzur River had turned reddish-brown and opaque, filled with sediment washed down from the hills.

We arrived drenched at Mr. Kaya's second-floor office, which looked out at the high-walled police compound. He was sixty-one, soft-voiced, and watchful. As we introduced ourselves, we could hear and see a police officer chatting on his phone at the window opposite. Mr. Kaya sat with his back to the wall, in a small pocket of privacy where he could not be seen through the tangled strip blinds. "I am used to being imprisoned for my democratic rights," he said. "Like protesting. Or talking to the press."

For his work, he had been twice detained, locked up, and tortured. His ribs had been broken, his face temporarily paralyzed down the left side. Dersim was a small town, so he often bumped into his torturers in the street. And yet he always returned here, to his office. Looking down at his hands in his lap, he calmly explained that he was currently awaiting another sentence. "If it is approved by the court I will go to prison for six years. I have never been involved in any sort of violent act; it is always for ideological reasons."

As Mr. Kaya had dedicated almost four decades to campaigning for public recognition of those persecuted and killed in Dersim, I wondered how he felt about President Erdoğan becoming the first government official to ever acknowledge and apologize for the massacres of 1937 and 1938. In a televised speech in 2011, Erdoğan described it as "one of the most tragic events in our recent history. It is a disaster that should now be questioned with courage." I was able to guess Mr. Kaya's feelings by the fact that Kerem could not ask the question without both of them laughing.

Like most people I met in Dersim, they understood Erdoğan's speech as an apology only to the extent that it allowed him to blame someone else. For their role in the killings he criticized his opposition—the CHP, the party of Atatürk and İnönü—while holding aloft military documents on which their names were signed. This quietly ignored the fact that, under his presidency, Dersim remained a police state. He was apologizing for a past that had not passed—and received a standing ovation. But to even comment on this contradiction was, as Mr. Kaya put it, "always a reason to go to prison."

I was planning to give him a copy of the document I had in my backpack—Siegfried's letter, dated April 1937. I thought it might make a contribution, however small, to the growing evidence of what happened here. Ever since speaking to Professor Akçam, I had even held on to the idea that my letter might be quietly revolutionary, the decisive rupture through which the truth would come rushing in. *The breakthrough that fills the vacuum.* Standing there in Mr. Kaya's office, his walls postered with the faces of the unremembered, his torturers also his neighbors, I began to understand the absurdity of thinking that all they needed was just more evidence.

For the last ten years, he had been helping to translate—from Zazaki, his mother tongue—some of the eight hundred hours of witness statements from the survivors of the massacres. "During the days when I work on them, I always have to take breaks to calm down and let my feelings out," he said. "Because what I have to translate is unbearable, emotionally . . . I worry about how this is changing my psychology." He was not the first person to talk about the side effects of such work. In Istanbul, I had met Cemal Taş—a man who single-handedly recorded an extensive archive of Dersimi oral histories—and he described how his children miss the person he was before he started his work.

"I know I have to do this," Mr. Kaya told me. He turned now to Metin and Kerem. "I am hopeful that the generations to come will let all the people around the world hear."

I did not get Siegfried's letter out of my bag. With a profound sense of avoidance, I decided it would be simpler to email it later. And perhaps Mr. Kaya sensed the thing I was unwilling to speak about because, after I'd asked my last question and thanked him for his time, he said, quite suddenly: "If your great-grandfather was involved in this massacre, this genocide—if he had any single role in this genocide—we forgive him." I had to listen back to the interview recording afterward to even be sure that I'd said it, a clogged sound from the back of the throat. *Thank you.* Even less audible was the embrace he gave me, reduced on tape to the *shush shush* of our clothes moving against each other, the synthetic fabrics coming together and then pulled apart.

6.

Back through town, we followed Metin and Kerem as they stepped wide around the many police officers and soldiers, as one might steer clear of a pothole. We got back to the truck and Metin drove us down the steep hill and along the river to where he runs his own business. Raised on stilts overlooking the water stood a wooden structure like an old Wild West saloon. This was the restaurant and bar he'd built himself, which was busy every summer with families eating and swimming and leaping into the river from an extremely dubious zip line. Inside the bar, a living tree burst through the floor and out the ceiling. Another tree pushed through the end of the bar, this one already in leaf. Only now did I pluck up the courage to ask Metin about his tattoo. He seemed a little surprised that I even knew about it, perhaps forgetting that it's one of the images that comes up when you google his name.

"What do the tourists think when they see it?"

"Those who don't know about my life, they're shocked," he said. "They think I'm a military man."

He admitted that it was not, after all, inspired by a mountain so much as an actual Kalashnikov. One of his friends in the PKK spent two days working on it. Metin said he chose the image because this was a time in his life when "you only trust your gun."

Like all young men in Turkey, Metin was required to do military service for the Turkish army. He knew his ongoing refusal to do so would eventually result in another prison sentence, probably longer than the last one. But he also knew that he could not join an army with its history or stand alongside the same soldiers that now looked down at him from the hills.

On the drive back, Metin pulled into a gas station. "We need to stop for gas," he said. Kerem turned to me and said, "As long as it's not poison gas." My laughter came out weird and loud, the kind of sound that makes everyone else stop laughing.

That night, we went to a restaurant by the river, where the white tablecloths were scattered with rose petals. It was Valentine's Day. Everywhere were couples holding hands, and Metin and Kerem seemed to know them all. Directly outside the window the Munzur still ran high from the rains and the restaurant had turned on its mood lights, so the water flowed green.

7.

After three days in the mountains, Eleanor and I caught the sleeper back to Ankara. On Mr. Kaya's advice, I sent Siegfried's letters to the Dersim History and Culture Center—an organization dedicated to documenting and seeking justice for the massacres—which is, by necessity, not based anywhere near Dersim. For now, it is run from Germany, and largely by volunteers.

In 2019 a group of German MPs put a question to the Bundestag: Did the German government not have a responsibility to fully explore and acknowledge its role in supplying weapons and expertise used in the Dersim massacres? The German government acknowledged "the suffering of the [Dersim] victims and their descendants" and said they were willing to examine German participation, but only once Turkey admitted that it had happened in the first place.

I found no mention of it in Siegfried's letters nor any further notes about the purchase of chemical weapons. If he knew anything about what happened in Dersim, he kept it off the page and also out of his memoir. All I did notice was that 1937 was not a good period for his health. He suffered from "chronic suppuration of the tonsils" that made it painful to eat.

Before I left Ankara, I tried once more to find a connection to where my family lived. I maneuvered my way into the staff room of a six-story language school and, with the help of a Turkish-speaking friend, explained that eighty years ago my family had, maybe, lived in an apartment block that had been, conceivably, not far from here. The dozen young teachers on their lunch break did not demand to know more. But they did let me stand in the top-floor café where, from the rear terrace, I looked out at the dingy backs of nearby offices and, with some effort, imagined that the nearly sweet smell of the bins far below was the scent rising from the apricot trees in the Merzbachers' back garden. On his balcony, Siegfried sat with his typewriter, keeping Professor Quasebart updated. By the end of 1938, he was finally no longer an employee of Auer and his wages were being paid exclusively by the Turkish Red Crescent, and even then he kept in touch. The professor's final visit to Ankara was in the summer of 1939. The latest issue of *Die Gasmaske* showed him receiving an award for Auer's "excellent achievements" as a "National Socialist model company."

In the end it was the onset of war—rather than any decisive action of his own—that finally severed Siegfried's relations with his old colleagues in Berlin. He and his family were vacationing on a Turkish steamer when they heard the news that German tanks had rolled into Poland. While the boat puttered past fishing villages on the Black Sea, they all gathered round the radio.

Within a year they were contacted by the German embassy in Ankara to inform them that their citizenship had been revoked.

On September 30, 1940, they handed in their passports. The word *ausgebürgert!!*—expatriated—would later be scrawled diagonally across their documents, then double underlined in red.

Siegfried wrote desperate letters to his connections in the Turkish government, asking to be granted citizenship, pitching his unique skill set, his years of "varied experience" as a chemist, and his "fiercest desire to devote all my knowledge to the benefit of the Turkish state and the Turkish nation." While they did not offer him statehood, he was given a more tenuous form of security. They renewed his contract at the gas mask factory.

V.

Your Very Devoted Servant

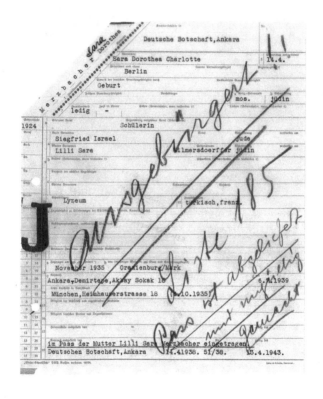

1.

In 1942, Ankara was somewhere that stateless Jews, fervent Nazis, and German political outcasts could all live on the same street. Turkey had managed to maintain its precarious neutrality even while surrounded by nations at war. Franz von Papen, the man who helped put Hitler in power, lived in the city as the German ambassador. In March, he survived a suicide bomb attempt while out for his morning stroll and it was an exiled German-Jewish doctor who treated his ruptured eardrums. My grandmother remembered she and her brother playing tennis on a court next to Papen's daughter. She said they sometimes spoke to her, "but never in a friendly way."

By now, Siegfried understood exactly how lucky they were to have landed in the Turkish capital. Through letters, he had heard news of his extended family in Germany: his brother-in-law's internment in Dachau, both sisters, Elisabeth and Luise, forced to flee the country. His cousin Alice deported to Theresienstadt, from where she never came back. Other family members who stayed behind took their own lives rather than risk the same fate. His cousin Franz overdosed on sleeping pills. His niece gassed herself with a kitchen stove.

Even as newspapers began to report on the extermination camps, Turkey retained its neutrality. It was not until August 5, 1944, that Siegfried wrote to his sister Elisabeth: "the Nazis are leaving." Turkey had broken off diplomatic relations and, overnight, all non-Jewish German citizens were given ten days to leave—or face internment. Again, Siegfried realized their good fortune: a world of opposites where suddenly everyone wanted a red *J* stamped in their passports. "Now people who hushed up their Jewish descent loudly proclaim their Jewishness!" Siegfried wrote to his sister. "Götterdämmerung!"

The majority of Germans tried to remain, preferring Turkish internment over a return to Nazi Germany. But there were different reasons for feeling this way: some wanted to stay because they opposed Hitler's racist regime and some because they worried that Hitler's racist regime was not going to win. This was a nuance irrelevant to the Turkish authorities, who rounded up all two hundred and interned them together in the quiet Anatolian town of Kırşehir. Siegfried wrote: "For our friends the worst thing is that they—always upright opponents of the Nazis—are thrown together with the Nazis in one pot."

Through these years, Siegfried's letters reveal his queasy recognition of their "unheard-of luck." They had good friends. He kept his job. His wife could still play Mendelssohn on her German-made piano. His son got a physics degree from the University of Istanbul. His daughter had been "very clever" in solving the problem of her statelessness. She was engaged to a Scotsman. And when Turkey did join the Allies in February 1945, there was little risk of bombs falling on Ankara, as the war was all but over.

My grandmother married my grandfather on VE Day, when

the whole city was celebrating and billowing with flags. This was a glorious backdrop for a marriage that was, in my mother's romantic phrasing, "a shotgun wedding of convenience"—a means to a British passport. The registrar signed their documents in the embassy stairwell, then went off to a party. Siegfried wrote that "Our children and grandchildren will live in a better world than we."

The following summer, he was standing on his balcony, holding a letter with a Berlin postmark. After seven years of silence, Professor Quasebart had got back in touch, just casually wondering how everything had gone in Ankara, but also describing his own wartime experiences in the German capital, the bombings, the Russian occupation, his valuables destroyed, his wife fleeing to Switzerland, brutal winters in a single room, the stroke he suffered just before the city fell which meant he could now no longer speak. Siegfried, sitting above the orchard where thousands of apricots hung in the trees, read the letter, but did not reply to it.

A month later, though, a second message arrived from Professor Quasebart—and this time he got straight to the point: "I need your help." He had lost his job as part of the Allied plan to "denazify" Germany. Although he did not mention it in his letter, the British military government in Berlin had singled him out for his company's use of forced labor from concentration camps as well as his pro-Nazi publications. But he was appealing the decision and needed references. As he pointedly reminded Siegfried: "It has always been a great relief to me that you were able to leave the country in good time, escaping the terrible things."

Siegfried went to his typewriter.

That was why I visited the Landesarchiv in the north of Berlin.

In a redbrick hangar, hundreds of thousands of denazification documents were laid out on miles of temperature-controlled roller shelves. I sat down with Professor Quasebart's file: a bulging stack of court transcripts, witness statements—and letters of support from old colleagues.

2.

The January of 1947 in Berlin was the coldest in living memory. Pipes and toilets froze, while bomb craters filled with snow. People lived beneath the rubble for warmth. The forests were stripped bare for kindling as the frost crept inside the houses, the walls of bedrooms glittering. Those who had not yet burned their National Socialist literature did so now.

It was seven degrees below freezing on the morning Professor Quasebart walked into the Tiergarten criminal court with its swirling double staircases, vertiginous ceilings, and a statue of Lady Justice. It was now an arm of the British military government. Quasebart was one of two hundred thousand senior figures who had been sacked or refused reemployment in the British zone.

In courtroom number one, he stood stiff and silent in his round-rimmed glasses, looking out at the five members of the denazification committee. At his side was his fifty-six-year-old housekeeper, Hedda, who explained that, as a result of his stroke, she would be speaking on his behalf. "I have known Professor Quasebart for about twenty years and have his very special trust," she said. "I know that he completely rejected National Socialism from the very first day. He always expressed his outrage at the persecution of the Jews."

Like millions of German citizens across the country, he had completed a denazification questionnaire. Anyone who wanted to have a role in the country's future had to fill one out and be marked on a five-point scale of guilt—from "major offender" to "exonerated." The form itself was comprehensive and occasionally absurd, requiring the applicant's name, height, weight, hair color, eye color, any "scars, birthmarks or deformities," and—after more than a hundred questions covering religion, military service, voting record, foreign travel, and family history—all their publications and speeches, which for Quasebart was a significant number. On extra sheets, he listed dozens of his scientific papers including civic-minded articles like "Can Citizens Be Protected against Warfare Agents?"

The court prosecutor had managed to find only some of the publications Quasebart conveniently forgot. He had obtained a copy of the *Auerspiegel*—the company magazine that took over from *Die Gasmaske*—and he held up the cover: a swastika beneath a silhouette of smokestacks. Underlined in red were a number of statements made in the professor's name, such as: "We are necessary members of a great organism that has important tasks to fulfill in the service of our people, our fatherland and our Führer."

The professor's housekeeper said that although he had signed off on these messages, they were written by his codirector, the "very fanatical" Robert Vorbau. In fact, she said, the statements would have been far more extreme if the professor had not "often grabbed the pen, changed it." She told the court that he had protected his Jewish colleagues. It was Vorbau who had pushed for Auer to be named a National Socialist "model company." It was Vorbau who created the newsletter. And since Vorbau was conveniently locked up or possibly dead in Sachsenhausen, he could not answer these charges.

Hedda then read out letters of unwavering support. Among them was Siegfried's. "From the beginning of the National Socialist regime, Professor Dr. Karl Quasebart did everything he could to ease my difficult situation. My family and I owe him our existence and our rescue from destruction." There was no mention of the nature of their work together. In Germany at the time, these kinds of immaculate character references were nicknamed "Persilscheine" after the popular detergent. They made everything come out clean.

A month later, Professor Quasebart received the news that, while the committee agreed he had gone out of his way to support certain Jewish colleagues, this was overshadowed by the enslaved laborers employed in his name, some of whom were beaten in the streets. His appeal was rejected.

He was bed-bound for much of the following year. A note from his doctor described "a significant increase in blood pressure" that required "extensive bloodletting. . . . The X-ray shows a dilated heart with a maximum configuration of the aorta, that is a cor bovinum." His heart was now three times its normal weight. *Cor bovinum*: cow's heart.

In the spring of 1948, and despite his poor health, Quasebart had not given up on clearing his name. One reason the British Military Government was attractive to those with questionable histories was the depth of its bureaucracy—and so he appealed the result of his failed appeal. While waiting for another court date, he had plenty of time to build his case, write letters, and call in favors. He was fortunate, too, that the British were growing tired of their role as moral saviors. There was now a cold-eyed understanding that, in order to get things done, they'd probably need a few mid-level Nazis to keep the country ticking over. There had also been complaints in the British press about the cost of the twenty-six thousand military bureaucrats required to run their portion of Germany. In April 1948, a new minister was brought in to oversee the zone, a Catholic aristocrat called Lord Pakenham, who told the House of Lords that denazification was a "horrid tiresome business" and that people "in Germany today, on all levels . . . are deeply conscious of their sad heritage." (That was a year before an opinion poll in the newly created West Germany found that 60 percent thought Nazism was a "good idea badly carried out.")

By the time Quasebart had his final hearing in September 1948, the British had all but abandoned their plan to purify Germany. In room 138, the prosecution brought no witnesses; the defense had ten. Quasebart had now built up a stack of positive references from all around the world, including one from Otto Hahn, "the father of nuclear chemistry," fresh from a Nobel Prize for discovering fission. Even the court interpreter translating the German discussion into English for the British bureaucrats' consideration did her part to clean up the professor's past. In a statement that Auer's "gas masks were not only delivered to the German military," her transcription left out the word "only."

With the help of Hedda, his formidable housekeeper, Quasebart led the committee through his references, including Siegfried's, with many of the statements read aloud by the chairman of the commission:

"Quasebart left no stone unturned to keep my Jewish husband, the engineer Karl Wollin, in his position as department head of the Auergesellschaft until the ever more ruthless enforcement of the Nuremberg Laws made this impossible." "His help was crucial in realizing my family's emigration plans in 1938/39 . . . I would like to demonstrate the consistent pro-Jewish attitude of Prof. Quasebart." ". . . in October 1944, he was the one who immediately used his extensive connections to save me from being deported to one of the 'labor camps.' Now that the roles have been exactly reversed today, I consider it my natural duty to stand up for Prof. Quasebart in public. It would be a mockery to identify this man alongside the Nazi criminals whose aims he fought and condemned at all times."

In my research I found documents that back up at least some of these claims. A confidential letter from Heinrich Himmler's office in 1939 showed that they considered him "politically unreliable" for his continued employment of, by their count, twelve Jews, four of whom were in management. I also confirmed that he had helped a number of Jewish colleagues and their families leave the country— including, of course, Siegfried. He also never joined the Nazi Party, despite pressure to do so.

But what was also true was that he remained a passionate militarist whose career thrived under the Nazis. He facilitated the country's ever-growing stockpiles of chemical weapons. He lectured at Auer's Gas Protection School, where SS troops were trained in how to use a modified variant of Zyklon B. This version of the pesticide had no "warning agent," a smell that would alert people to its presence. Obviously this made using the gas much more dangerous, but it was a necessary adjustment when using it to kill humans. His company supplied the gas masks necessary to carry out the industrial murder of those about whose persecution he said he had "always expressed his outrage."

Perhaps Siegfried sent a glowing letter of support in part because these were contradictions to which he could relate. Or perhaps he sent the letter for the simple reason that he owed his boss a favor—given how lucky they had been to spend the war in Ankara.

After a brief deliberation, the appeal court's verdict was unanimous. Professor Quasebart was recommended for exoneration, but he died six months later, his case still in process.

What struck me most about reading the hundreds of pages of transcripts in Quasebart's denazification file was that only one witness was ever asked about chemical weapons. He was Dr. Gerdes, a former codirector from Auer and an SS member since 1934. He and Quasebart had worked together extensively and were both board members at Orgacid.

"Do you know if the appellant was interested in making poison gas?" the chairman asked.

"No," Gerdes said, "nothing was done with poison gases."

The records noted: *Quasebart could not speak.*

3.

In the summer of 2021, I was given an opportunity to talk publicly about my family history. I had been invited to deliver a speech at Berlin's House of Representatives, the state parliament. In truth, I had actually been asked to talk about my grandmother's life but, given my recent research, I wanted to acknowledge the wider complexities and mention my great-grandfather's work, if not go further and admit that, in a sense, our family's escape from Nazi Germany was, I imagined myself saying, predicated on complicity, and wasn't it vital that here, today, in the heart of government, we should feel able to recognize such ambiguities because how else will we ever see one another as fully human? These were the kinds of sentences that I began to repeat, internally, as I paced back and forth in my study, trying to work out how I would fit all my brave and profoundly insightful sentiments into my allotted ten minutes.

The speech was to mark the reopening of an exhibition featuring my grandmother. I had already been to see it when it was on at Berlin's central synagogue. That was before I started writing this book, and I was given a private tour by the curator. I remember becoming aware of a gruesome sense of celebrity. In a vaulted room in one of the ornate onion-shaped domes, I was photographed beside a life-size image of my grandmother, even as I had the thought that, by her own admission, she never set foot in a synagogue.

As I now tried to write my speech, I reread the exhibition catalogue and its potted biography of my grandmother's life, how "her Jewish family escaped Nazi persecution when her father, a chemist, was posted to Turkey by the company he worked for." Was ten minutes long enough to even unpack the words "the company he worked for"? Could I expand those words to include the chemical weapons laboratory by the river, the bunkers of Orgacid, and how he remained Quasebart's man in Ankara, facilitating the delivery of chemical weapons for the Turkish government?

I looked up pictures of the House of Representatives. It was an imposingly columned building on Niederkirchnerstrasse, and I read about how the architects had approached the brief with "the principle of layering"—seeking to acknowledge the property's previous uses as the Prussian parliament, a Nazi aviation ministry, and offices for Soviet East German bureaucrats. This was, I told myself, somewhere expressly designed to sustain ambiguity. And yet in practicing my speech out loud, I found there was a significant difference between the words I could write on paper and those that I was willing to say out of my own personal mouth. As I imagined the rows of dignitaries listening to me, I found myself using gentler phrases. Perhaps my Jewish great-grandfather did not so much *manufacture* chemical weapons as find himself in a position where he was working on them, obliged by the oppressive circumstances of the time to oversee a laboratory whose true military intentions he could never have foreseen and which weighed heavily on him for the rest of his life. I realized that—among my rows of imagined politicians—there were the representatives of Alternative für Deutschland, Germany's resurgent right-wing populist party. Berlin's mayor, Michael Müller, had written that if the AfD got double figures in the last city elections, in 2016, it would be "seen around the world as a sign of the return of the right-wing and the Nazis in Germany." That was shortly before they won 14.2 percent of the seats.

In the end, I wrote a speech in which I spoke exclusively about my grandmother's life because, I decided, that was what was expected of me, and it would simply be inappropriate to mention all the things I really didn't want to mention. Pandemic restrictions meant that I never stepped inside the House of Representatives and the speech had to be delivered over Zoom. Even then, from the safety of my own study, hundreds of miles away from Berlin, I could not bring myself to make anyone uncomfortable. I opened my speech in German—*Es ist schön, heute mit euch allen zusammen zu sein*—that being the first of three sentences I practiced a dozen times with my mother, resulting in a deeply misleading impression of my fluency in the language. I could not even tell you the precise meaning of what I was saying—only that it was very polite. I talked through my grandmother's life, from radioactive toothpaste, to the swastika being raised above her school, to their escape into Turkey—and how, many decades later, she returned to Berlin to tell her story. I ended by saying that my mother, my sisters, and I were now in the process of being "renaturalized" as German citizens, "the restoration of a previous relationship, not the start of a new one. . . . Exhibitions like this one remind us to see beyond the borders that divide us, to see past labels and locate our common humanity." These were words so bland you could barely hear them. It was only in the ninth and final minute of my speech that I attempted some acknowledgment of the unsaid:

My grandmother would not want the story of her life to end with neat closure or catharsis. She herself was full of contradictions, capable of being funny and warm and brutal and spiky, often all during the one game of Scrabble. I know that she would be very glad to see this exhibition, to have her experiences so powerfully remembered. But I also know that she would be the first to comment on what had been missed or got wrong. I can only imagine what funny and damning things she would say to me, having listened to my attempt to squeeze her whole life into a ten-minute speech. I wish she were still here to say it.

After slapping shut the laptop, I felt a strange blend of adrenaline and shame, mixed with the sudden aloneness that follows the end of video calls. The corkboard above my desk was pinned, in the manner of a TV homicide detective, with copies of some of the photos and documents that were central to my research. As I sat there, I read again the reference that Siegfried had written for his old boss in 1946: "From the beginning of the National Socialist regime, Professor Dr. Karl Quasebart did everything he could to ease my difficult situation." In his unblinking letter of support I recognized a kindred form of cowardice. He was careful, as I was, to tell only one part of the story. It would have just been rude, wouldn't it, for either of us to mention the industrial production of poisonous gases? We weren't lying, he and I. We were simply fulfilling the brief.

Also on the corkboard was Siegfried's confession about his work with chemical weapons, pinned up there after my copy of the memoir began to disintegrate. I often referred to these few pages, so they were annotated and crinkled and, after one incident, stained so heavily with tea that it gave them a look of hard-won authenticity, as though they had lain buried in the earth.

> Now I come to the darkest chapter of my professional life. . . . Today I confess to my descendants who will read these lines that I made a grave error. I have betrayed myself, my most sacred principles. Although I had some outward successes and some comforts, I fell into a severe depression for many years. And even today, that part of my past weighs on me. . . . I cannot shake off the great debt on my conscience.

Looking at it again now I felt I recognized something else. I heard in those words my own smoothed-over tone, as of someone speaking to an inner jury. These felt like the kinds of sentences you might practice in the mirror. If the narrator of the memoir was the ideal part of himself, then where had Siegfried hidden the rest?

I knew that my great-grandfather had been "briefly hospitalized" at a psychiatric unit in North Carolina in 1957. In an introduction to the English translation of the memoir, his son mentioned that Siegfried had "begun to suffer from a malady known as a 'retirement depression.'" According to Eugen, this was not the result of anything so grandiose as a moral debt, but was simply the comedown after a long and busy career. It was hard to know what to do with these incompatible versions of his mental state: one in which he never recovered from the guilt of producing chemical weapons for a genocidal regime and the other in which he just needed a hobby.

As I listened to the soothing, interplanetary hold music of Ciox—the corporation that stores most medical records in America—I did not hold out much hope of finding an answer. After half an hour of waiting, a polite man took my great-grandfather's details and asked me to confirm again the birth year: 1883. This was, he noted, a time before the motorcar, the tone of his voice suggesting that I should probably move on with my life. He eventually confirmed that some medical records did exist but, when I admitted that I wasn't, strictly speaking, the next of kin, the call ended quickly. I then set up a fake email account in my mother's name and wrote to Ciox from there. I received no reply.

When I told my mother all this, she said that I fundamentally failed to understand the nature of American bureaucracy. Four weeks later, she had struck up a lifelong friendship with the woman in the hospital's records office. Across multiple phone calls they had formed a bond sufficient enough that the woman had happily descended into a distant basement, retrieved and copied the microfiche, and a week later it all arrived by airmail at my parents' house in Wales, free of charge: forty-five pages of observations, notes, sleep charts, medication records, and Freudian analysis from the autumn of 1957. As soon as my mother had finished reading it, she phoned me, and the first thing she said, with a note of disapproval, was: "You're going to be very happy."

VI.

Equanimity

1.

It started with his teeth. In the summer of 1955, his American dentist suggested full extraction and dentures as a solution to Siegfried's long-standing discomfort. There was no record of whether they discussed his history with radioactive toothpaste or the time he voluntarily injected his gums with radium-228. Either way there were good reasons to think Siegfried's teeth might require an intervention.

He and Lilli were now living in Newark, New Jersey. They had followed their son to America, where his career was taking off. After completing his degree in Istanbul, Eugen had received his MA and PhD from Harvard, and was now working at the Institute for Advanced Study in Princeton. His colleagues included the institute's director, J. Robert Oppenheimer, as well as Albert Einstein, who described Princeton as "a wonderful little spot, a quaint and ceremonious village of puny demigods on stilts."

While his son was moving among deities, Siegfried found work at a New Jersey paint factory. He was now seventy-two years old, smoked unfiltered Chesterfields, and was bald but for a wreath of fine gray hair. His boss was Dr. Stern, a man who had been, thirty years earlier, one of the less promising young assistants at Auer. Siegfried felt humiliated by their switched roles. His primary memory of their time together in Oranienburg was the day that Stern volunteered to test a fabric against mustard gas and his whole forearm came up in blisters like bubble wrap. Siegfried had noticed that his young boss now seemed to take pleasure in making him uncomfortable. And during those long afternoons in Newark, told to stand over a churning vat of resin, another methylene chloride headache grinding behind his eyeballs, the thought of his son striding across swaths of perfect lawn, discussing the collapse of dying stars with a group of Nobel laureates, provoked some unfatherly feelings.

In the summer of 1952, Stern had insisted Siegfried research a new product, a radioluminescent paint that would out-glow its competitors. He was told to experiment with radioactive strontium, known for its "bone-seeking" isotopes that gather in the teeth. Siegfried considered the project unsafe—his attitude having changed since the days of radioactive toothpaste—but nevertheless he did what he was told.

At the end of each day, he and Lilli walked home together through the warehouses and smokestacks of Newark. She was a secretary at a neighboring firm, the Gold Leaf & Metallic Powders Company, making use of her superior English. When they sometimes stopped at one of the German-Jewish shops to buy something for dinner, they had to be careful, though: they got suspicious looks for sounding too German. Finally they ascended the stairs to their cramped fourth-floor apartment with its tiny metal balcony on which there was just space enough to stand and peer out, not at the majestic view across the water to the Manhattan skyline, but rather at the airport and swamps.

Despite the dentist's recommendation, Siegfried could not bring himself to have his teeth removed. His fear of anesthetic stemmed from a bad experience in Oranienburg. An anesthetist had put him to sleep with insufficient ether and he regained consciousness in the middle of the operation, his arms and legs strapped down with belts. He started writhing, screaming, and also hallucinating, suddenly certain that the doctor standing over him with a scalpel was one of his own lab assistants. Though it had all happened decades and continents ago, this terror returned to him with every visit to the dentist.

In the end, Siegfried agreed to have the dentures fitted just to get it over with—the anticipation of possible surgery proving as traumatic as the procedure itself. The two operations went well, and yet his new teeth pinched and rubbed and, when they weren't in his mouth, provided a vision of his own death, grinning at him from a glass on his bedside table. He began to fear that his whole body was failing him, and this fear led to further complications. He had never experienced impotency before. In fact, he had always thought of himself as largely nonsexual, certainly not someone whose self-esteem was linked to his sex life. Only after erections were no longer available to him did he concede that they had been, after all, quite significant.

In the summer of 1956, he spoke to the family doctor about his listlessness, his anxiety, his problems in the bedroom, his sense of impending death, and was reassured that this was a common response to retirement. He had recently quit his job at the paint factory. After seven years spent mixing lacquers and resins, he said he "could no longer tolerate it." In the meantime, Eugen had been made professor of physics at the University of North Carolina so, at his invitation, Siegfried and Lilli moved to a pretty ground-floor flat in a leafy part of Chapel Hill, where they would, in theory, embrace a slower pace of life, take walks in the arboretum, and spend time with the grandkids.

In practice, Siegfried started to think there was something seriously wrong with him. It was at its worst in the mornings, when he felt weighed down, his eyes prickling, forever on the edge of tears that never came. He had been in and out of therapy for almost half his life, beginning with Dr. Heinrich Koerber in Berlin, a committed Freudian, complete with couch, beard, and pipe. Then it was Dr. Edgar Michaelis, known for his work on human duality, or how we wear masks to hide our true selves. (Michaelis argued that the entire practice of Freudian therapy was, itself, an elaborate cover for the unresolved pain of its founder.) Then, years later, when Siegfried arrived in America, he sometimes caught the train from Newark into Manhattan to see a shrink. In other words, Siegfried had enough experience of anxiety and depression to notice that this time felt different.

His doctor prescribed him meprobamate, a tranquilizer, the advert for which promised calm seas: *for equanimity.* Thus he joined the millions of Americans who needed something to take the edge off. Under the brand names Miltown and Equanil, meprobamate had become the bestselling drug in America, the world's first blockbuster psychotropic, beloved of Hollywood stars, who were known to drink "miltinis," vermouth and vodka with a pill instead of an olive. It was an open question as to whether this treatment did anything to tackle the underlying problem or if it merely, in Freudian terms, masked it. Studies soon showed that meprobamate was habit-forming, while it also carried the risk of a wide range of side effects, from jaundice to trembling to—in rare cases—suicidal depressions. For his part, Siegfried found that the pills gave him a calmness that verged on stupor, while not addressing the more or less constant feeling that he was about to die.

By the spring of 1957, his anxiety had widened so that whenever Lilli went out, even to the grocery store, he was overcome with the certainty that she would not come back alive. If Ann, his highly capable daughter-in-law, was a few minutes late to meet him, he believed that she had been in a fatal collision. He tried to control his fears by willpower alone, taking long walks on the trails through Battle Park or by furious housework, washing dishes as though trying to drown them, but these tactics became less and less effective.

In June that year, he got a phone call informing him that his nephew and family had been in a non-imaginary car accident. The children had cuts and bruises, but the parents had been hospitalized, his nephew with a broken leg. There had been a head-on with a truck, its driver asleep at the wheel. And then, a month later, he was sitting reading the paper on the porch in Chapel Hill when he saw a small report about a large earthquake, the epicenter of which was near Tehran. His daughter—my grandmother—was living there with her husband and three children; my mother was eleven at the time. I couldn't track down the exact headline that Siegfried read, but I got a sense of it from British newspapers on the same day: "Over 1,000 Killed in Earthquake. Persian Villages Turned into Cemeteries." Described by the *Times* as "the most severe within memory," the earthquake happened at night, so the victims were crushed in their beds.

His body was in terminal decay. Truck drivers nodded off at the wheel. Buildings collapsed on sleeping children. These were not inventions of an overactive mind. And yet those around him seemed capable of ignoring the oblivion that was waiting behind every door. Siegfried folded his newspaper, stubbed out his cigarette, walked into the apartment, and began bashing his head against the wall. He kept going for several minutes, as though trying to bring the building down around him, and as he did so, he yelled what he would later call "nonsense," but that according to his medical report "consist[ed] of statements to the effect that he should die and that he cannot go on any longer and must die."

It was a few days before his daughter could communicate that she and her children had safely hidden beneath the big dining table in their two-story house on a hill suburb of Tehran, watching the pictures rattle on the walls; as my mother told me, she found the earthquake "rather exciting." Meanwhile, Siegfried's son had taken him to see a psychoanalyst, a Jewish and German-born woman, Dr. Lucie Jessner, who wore a shirt with a pattern of bloodred polka dots that revealed themselves to be, on closer inspection, little strawberries. Like her patient, she had escaped Nazi Germany and ended up in America. Unlike him, she had a sunny disposition and was now professor of psychiatry at the University of North Carolina School of Medicine. In retrospect, it was perhaps not such a good idea for Siegfried to seek solace from someone who had achieved everything he had not. In their interview he told her that, during the war, he had "got a professorship in Istanbul." This was the life he would have liked for himself, not the one he actually lived. He made no mention of his decade on low pay making gas masks for the Turkish military.

He was honest about his fears, though, the most persistent of which was the constant expectation that he and his loved ones were about to die. The doctor wrote: "In the early morning he is grasped by such fear that he cannot contain himself, hits his head against the wall, cries that he has to kill himself. He despises himself for such behavior because he tortures his wife with it. The only way out seems death." She noted a "moderate danger of suicide." Death, by his logic, was the cure to the fear of itself.

He told the doctor how, on the wall of the childhood bedroom he shared with his sisters in Munich, there had been a large and terrifying oil painting of their great-grandfather, Jizhak Merzbacher, the furrier, with his black yarmulke and straggly white beard. The artist had done little to hide that this was a posthumous portrait, the shrunken and ash-gray death head of their ancestor bearing down on them in their beds as they slept. As a child, Siegfried knew the story of Jizhak's death, how he had met his end the night a huge fire tore through his town. The important detail, though, was that Jizhak's home had escaped the flames unharmed. He died, instead, of a "panic attack" while waiting for the fire to reach him. He died from a fear of dying.

When Dr. Jessner recommended Siegfried spend a few days on the in-patient unit, he refused. There was something about staying overnight that, for him, crossed a line. He said he'd prefer to just pop in during the daytime, keep it casual. A week later he was visited at home by his older sister, Elisabeth, who had flown over from Washington with her son. This was impressive because her agoraphobia meant she rarely went outside and, when she did, she needed help to cross the road. They had a pleasant week together but, on the day that Elisabeth packed her bags to leave, Siegfried started to get agitated. It was not a physical sensation—no shortness of breath, no pain or palpitations—just an overwhelming sense of "impending calamity" and the certainty that he could do nothing to stop it. He was sure that she was going to collapse on the doorstep or get sideswiped by a truck while driving to the airport or that a mid-flight engine fire would fill the cabin with noxious smoke. Again he rose from his seat and started beating his head against the wall, yelling now that he should—as the nurse would later write on his admissions letter—"throw himself under the first passing automobile."

2.

At 10:45 a.m. on Tuesday, September 10, 1957, Siegfried walked un-aided into the North Carolina Memorial Hospital's psychiatric unit. He was dressed smartly in his pressed gray slacks, button-up shirt, and thick-rimmed specs, looking more consultant than patient—although the nurse noted that his feet barely left the ground as he walked.

His first appointment was with the admissions nurse, Nancy Matthews, who gave him a full physical, noted his "teeth absent—well-fitting plates," listened to his lungs and heart, palpated his prostate, recorded the size of his penis and testicles, observed the crookedness in his left foot's third toe—and then interviewed him about his family and work history, his "premorbid personality," and his childhood. It was perhaps unsurprising, given where the nurse had put her fingers, that he did not feel chatty. When she asked Siegfried for his earliest memory, he apologized, saying he was "able to recall little of his early life." But over the ten days to come, he would go on to discuss almost every aspect of his personal history. In their notes, Siegfried's doctors broke his experience down into discrete themes—family, school, work, marriage—so that all the mess of his life was tidied up and given shape. It was only after I'd finished reading that I realized he had not once mentioned chemical weapons. In this private and confidential account for his doctors—as opposed to the public one he would pass down to his family in his memoir—there was no talk of the ethical millstone weighing him down, the unshiftable burden on his conscience. He was definitely withholding the truth from someone, I just wasn't sure who.

Family

"His mother expired in 1936 but this
did not seem to upset the patient."

His earliest memory was of his fourth birthday, waking up to watch his nanny light the lamps. He told his doctors he could not remember a life without the care of Anna Walter, their then fifty-two-year-old *Kinderfräulein*, whose catchphrase was "my head hurts so much that I could scream." She never considered her frequent migraines sufficient to have a day off or to loosen the gray hair she pinned tight above her head. She was short, thin, and made no secret of preferring sons to daughters, calling his sisters "the big" and "the small," while he, her favorite, was "Bobs." Siegfried loved her and thought of her as his "surrogate mother," which was notable given that his biological mother was usually sitting next door.

Looking back at his childhood, Siegfried understood that Anna had not been, objectively speaking, a good carer. She never took them outside and had no understanding of play—she kept all the toys on a high shelf and insisted that each one be cleaned and put away before a new one could be requested. Though the children were never less than obedient, she was needlessly strict, threatening to lock them in the coal shed if they misbehaved. And yet, she loved him and he loved her. All those years later, he could still hear her voice, her Silesian accent and certain strange turns of phrase, like her euphemism for a bowel movement.

Bobs, do you need to go and be joyful?

———

The duty nurse wrote that Siegfried "smiled and seemed forcefully pleasant" as she showed him to his bedroom on the second floor of the hospital's south wing. In fact, he remained cheerful for as long as she remained in his room but, the moment she stepped outside and shut the door, he "burst into tears."

After lunch, Siegfried stood at the front desk, holding the handset to his ear, listening to his wife not pick up. When Lilli and his son did eventually come to drop off his spare clothes and typewriter, the problem of their arriving was that it necessitated their leaving. As soon as they went away he sat sobbing on his bed, hiding his face in his hands.

———

His parents saw their children only at mealtimes, when Anna would herd Siegfried and his sisters out of the playroom and down the long dim corridor. They could feel, underfoot, the shift from thick, sticky linoleum to herringbone parquet as they reached the adult world, the dining room where the windows got bigger and the air stuffier—walls hung with swallowtail gas burners in milk-white globes. In the apartment's front rooms, with a famous view of the palace and the theater, everything was elegant and no one seemed happy. After dinner, there was a further thirty minutes in the company of their parents before Anna knocked at the door and their father—in a reference to *Don Giovanni* that the children didn't get—would say, "Here comes the Commendatore." In Mozart's opera, the Commendatore is a ghost who arrives to drag the sinful protagonist to hell or, in this case, bedtime.

———

When Dr. Rex Speers, a first-year resident in psychiatry, had his initial visit with Siegfried, he felt there was not much wrong with this "nice-smelling old man." They got on well, discussed the news, and the doctor noted that the patient "laughs often and with obvious pleasure" and was maybe only "a little depressed." But the good humor of their first session receded as they spent more time together, and the doctor wondered if, in retrospect, the patient might be "quite skillful in disguising his disability."

———

Siegfried was twenty years old when his father died, and he had detailed memories of that day. With his mother audibly sobbing in the next room, he had been alone beside the bed when the old man took his final and frighteningly vigorous breaths—three huge gulps before the body fell still. Siegfried's heart had been thumping in his chest, and yet he felt "strangely calm."

By contrast his mother's death, when he was forty-nine, had seemed to barely make a ripple. He told his doctors next to nothing about her. In his memoir she was a distant figure, deteriorating in a Bavarian sanatorium. He managed just one sentence about her funeral. "It took place in Munich and naturally I attended." Naturally.

Only the death of his nanny, Anna, when he was thirty-two, had made him feel what he was "supposed" to. She had been living in a musty care home on Arcisstrasse, her gray hair still tied tight on her head, and he recognized the smell of acetone as soon as he walked in—a sweet, cloying scent like marzipan, familiar from his laboratory work. Eventually, he'd realized that it was coming from her breath, a symptom of her type 1 diabetes. He was haunted by the knowledge that if she'd lived a little longer, her life could have been saved by science—with the invention of synthetic insulin. But on her deathbed she had been nearly blind, eyes bloodshot, the blue of her irises threaded with red. She had no money, but still she pressed a coin into his palm. As they spoke, he felt his own eyes well up and his vision swam. They sat there, trying to see each other.

Her body was laid behind glass in Munich's Northern Cemetery, surrounded by flowers. As a death-fearing child, Siegfried had always found open caskets horrifying, every archway with its own corpse in formal wear. But for her he swallowed his fears and walked past the rows of bodies, stood at her side and wept.

———

Every night in the hospital, Siegfried was encouraged to try and sleep without chemical assistance and every night he came out of his room to ask for chloral hydrate. A nurse supervised as he swallowed a pill that contained a chemical he'd once seen burning in a factory blaze back in Oranienburg, an all-night bonfire of sedatives. Then she watched him return to his bedroom and turn off the light.

School

"I gather the patient has never learned how to play…"

Siegfried told his doctors that he still dreamed of Max Hirschberg, his best friend from school. Sometimes in these dreams they would battle each other to get the highest marks. Sometimes he was back in the cold exam hall, all of his knowledge of Greek and Latin wiped from his mind, while sadistic Dr. Seibel smirked from the lectern. Siegfried would look over in horror to see Max's pen effortlessly gliding across the page.

———

They met on their first day at the Wilhelmsgymnasium—the oldest and most prestigious boys' school in Bavaria—both seated up front in the large assembly hall, breathing in the overripe smell of six hundred and fifty adolescents being forced to listen to a full recital of the disciplinary code. Punishments included spending time in a cell in the basement. Siegfried was relieved to immediately catch whooping cough and get sent home. He spent the next two days happily in bed, where Anna brought him mugs of stewed Icelandic moss to loosen the mucus.

Once he was back at school, he and Max sat together in the first row, top of their class in all subjects except gymnastics. Many of their classmates were the sons of barons, dukes, and cavalry generals—von Koenitz, von Hauch, the von Redwitz brothers—the *von* in their names indicating their nobility. These boys were treated differently, arriving at school in spurred riding boots, trailed by footmen in tailcoats. Each morning, Siegfried watched them pause outside the gates while their manservants held out baskets into which they placed their ceremonial swords before striding in unencumbered. At school they were officially known as the *Königliche Edelknaben*—literally, Royal Noble Boys—and privately known, to their non-von peers, as the *Königliche Eselknaben*, the Royal Donkey Boys. It was believed that, no matter how stupid they were, the boys with silver buttons on their tight blue jackets always passed their exams.

One particular day in their fourth year shaped the lives of both Max and Siegfried. Their class got a visit from a young royal prince, at whose arrival they were all required to stand and recite a patriotic poem, "Hurrah, Germania!" by Ferdinand Freiligrath. It was a work of 376 words, thirty-six of which were "hurrah." It had just two full stops and forty-nine exclamation marks. The poem was written in 1870, just days after the French declared war on Prussia, and it was an extended call to arms: *For German right, for German speech, / For German household ways, / For German homesteads, all and each, / Strike home through battle's blaze! / Hurrah! Hurrah! Hurrah! / Hurrah! Germania!*

The moment the dim-looking young prince left the classroom, the students burst out laughing. For Max, this was the first time he understood that openly questioning authority could be exhilarating. Thirty years later, he had become the leading defense lawyer in Munich's courts, a left-wing Jew in a system that was unashamedly conservative, speaking truth to power, overturning wrongful convictions and—against the advice of his colleagues, who feared, correctly, that he would make himself a target—taking on Hitler in court in 1929, making him so angry at being cross-questioned by "these Jewish lawyers" that, as one newspaper put it, he "foamed."

Hirschberg came to be regarded as one of the world's great wrongful conviction lawyers and was the subject of a weighty biography, which was where I found the anecdote about the young prince. There was only one mention of the boy who sat next to him at school, the supposed best friend, who was referred to as "a certain Narzbacher."

In Siegfried's recollection of the same day, he recited the poem so well his teacher chose him to read it again in front of the parents at the May Day feast. In the echoey school auditorium, he stood in front of not only his own parents but those of the noble boys, the dukes, colonels, and generals. He was so nervous that he felt they could all see straight through him, see his heart pounding in his chest, and yet he read the poem flawlessly, calling out to Mother Germany: *Hurrah! thou lady proud and fair, / Hurrah! Germania mine!*

————

During their third session, Dr. Speers "led him into" a series of verbalizations so that he might attain "a realization of his problem." This involved Siegfried sitting on his bed and saying out loud: "I feel that I want to do things but I am afraid to do them." Then "I can see that my problem is to mix with people, to do some light tasks and develop some hobbies but it is impossible for me to do these things." And finally: "I want to make friends with people but have always been so shy and timid that I am unable to make friends."

That evening the sofas and chairs in the dayroom were pushed back and the TV was wheeled away on its own little gurney as the orderlies prepared the space for the weekly dance. At 8 p.m., Siegfried came out of his room, nodded and smiled at the music, but stayed in his doorway, observing the other patients as they stepped out with various degrees of reluctance and stiffness. After a while, Nurse Matthews approached him, but her offer was "politely declined."

Siegfried watched for fifteen more minutes, then returned to his room and got into bed. A short while later, he rose to paper over the window in his door in order to keep the light from his eyes.

———

At their graduation ball in the Café Luitpold, Siegfried stood frozen at the edge of the room, watching Max and his other classmates spin their partners beneath a whole weather system of chandeliers. Beside him was his date, a Fräulein Einstein who, arms crossed, was slowly coming to terms with her mistake. Siegfried felt sorry for her, but no amount of sympathy could make him brave enough to take her hand. Decades later, he remembered the sensation of being locked inside his morning dress, how its cardboard cuffs, collar, and shirt breast felt like a suit of armor.

Over the years, he followed the blossoming of Max's career as an outspoken lawyer. After the Nazis came to power, his old friend was one of the first to be arrested and jailed. By that time, Siegfried was living in his large company apartment with its bomb shelter in the basement, working at a private laboratory by the river, and was sometimes woken in the mornings by the sound of prisoners walking past his windows.

Work

"Patient says he is feeling better now—typing."

Both Siegfried and the duty nurse agreed that the most effective treatment was his typewriter. For hours each day the nurses could hear him happily rattling away in his room, the evenings punctuated by the ringing of the margin bell. If the nurse asked what he was working on he would explain that he was redrafting a graduate textbook about quantum mechanics. This was the kind of statement that felt good to say out loud in a psychiatric setting. Less pleasing were the finer details: that he was actually working on his son's project, having been asked for help precisely because Eugen understood that his father needed to feel, in some way, important. Siegfried's role was essentially secretarial, typing up Eugen's handwritten pages so that they could be copied and shared with his students for feedback.

Whenever the text required an equation, Siegfried wrote them in by hand, using his immaculately spaced handwriting, the product of his classical education. Though he was by no means an expert on the subatomic, he knew enough to understand that his son's book was an approachable and friendly dismantling of the entire classical scientific belief system on which Siegfried's life had been built. Faith in objective and immutable truths—man's march toward ultimate and permanent clarity—had been revealed as an object lesson in human arrogance.

———

In the back room of the Ohel Jakob synagogue in Munich, Siegfried spent his thirteenth year memorizing long passages from Prophets.

Though the walls were lined with books his grandfather had donated, ornate Torah scrolls on vellum, he already had his doubts. During those long hours preparing for his bar mitzvah, he developed his own rationalist approach to his faith: "If the Orthodox doctrine is correct but I have abandoned the customs then I will be punished for eternity. If, on the other hand, the Orthodox beliefs are incorrect then I lose nothing by continuing Orthodox practice." He decided to keep on the right side of God, on the off chance that God existed. Faith as a form of probability.

His father was chairman of the synagogue, and Siegfried waited for him to die before he and his cousin Fritz took a trip to Würzburg with the specific intention of embracing their damnation. On the train there, Siegfried tried to eat a ham sandwich, but was surprised to find himself physically repelled. He spent the rest of the journey kneeling in the toilet, retching into the darkness. Days later, in a leafy garden restaurant in Hamburg harbor, Siegfried did manage to lift the fork to his lips and chew an overdone chop until his jaw muscles burned and all that remained was a row of gnawed but unswallowable bits of gristle lined up neatly at the edge of his plate. Then the sky grew suddenly dark.

This was, they knew, a partial solar eclipse that, by chance, coincided with their lunch hour. As such, he and Fritz were able to enjoy the theater of their righteous punishment, looking up in horror at the extinguished sun and instant nightfall, feeling the sudden chill; in fact, Siegfried thought that this eclipse, which had been announced in the morning papers, was proof, not of God, but of a knowable and measurable universe, the clockwork planets.

Freed from his father and grandfather's beliefs, he returned to his studies at the University of Munich. There, he felt fortunate to be lectured by Wilhelm Röntgen, one of his heroes, the man who discovered X-rays—a "new kind of light for the investigation of dark places." Siegfried always arrived early and got a front seat to compensate for the great man's mumbling. Standing stiffly behind the rows of glass beakers and flasks, Röntgen talked into his enormous beard, this revered professor with the soul of a lab technician, a man who often cared more about the equipment than about his colleagues, and who point-blank refused to re-create his famous experiment, which had forever changed the human perception of reality. Week by week, the attendance at his lectures thinned as students recognized that he was never going to choose a volunteer from the front row and reveal their living insides, show the heart pulsing in the chest like a jellyfish.

In Röntgen, Siegfried had found a role model and, from then on, he never let his studies be diluted by anything so frivolous as pleasure. He threw himself into his seminars, lectures, and long afternoons at the training laboratory on Lindwurmstrasse, his white coat tight over his suit jacket. It was here he had his first taste of chlorine gas. After heating manganese dioxide and concentrated hydrochloric acid, he practiced maintaining scholarly distance from its "suffocating odor."

———

On his fourth day at the hospital, Siegfried was taken down to the basement room, a red warning light above the door. A young radiographer asked Siegfried to remove his shirt, step between a lead screen and a photo plate, then take a deep breath and hold it.

The X-ray revealed holly leaf–shaped opacities in his lungs (due to asbestos exposure), mild pulmonary emphysema (a known symptom of mustard gas exposure), and spinal osteoporosis, all of which was to say that, for a seventy-four-year-old chain-smoking industrial chemist with his professional history, he was "in excellent health." The radiographer noted that his heart was "not considered to be enlarged."

Later that day, Professor Merzbacher—his son—stopped by the hospital to deliver more handwritten pages before heading off to give a lecture. Siegfried assured his doctors that he was unambiguously proud of his son's achievements and they did not remotely believe him.

Marriage

"He describes his marriage as having been perfect
in every respect."

In 1918, Siegfried was thirty-five, single, and living alone with his mother in the same Munich apartment in which he had spent almost his entire life. Lying awake one night, he mentally trawled through his memory, trying to recall the "few women of marriageable age whom I knew." That was how he arrived at Lilli. She was single at twenty-five, which made her, in his words, "a leftover." He had met her properly only once, years ago, at one of her father's Thursday night soirees, and though they spoke only briefly then and made no meaningful eye contact across the room, he now felt, lying alone in his bedroom, that there had, after all, been a connection. "In retrospect she appeared to me such a fine, good-hearted and lovable person that I became interested in approaching her." Few words set the heart alight like "in retrospect." Their friends arranged for them to meet at the Grand Hotel Continental and, when he saw her walking toward him across the lobby—his heart full of feelings for the person that he had decided she was—he "immediately knew."

They were married in the garden of her father's house, a grand eccentric villa on the moneyed side of the river. It had turrets and battlements, and spikes above the gate, embodying a neo-Gothic longing for the simpler days of feudal law. On his way to the ceremony, in his coattails, Siegfried passed a flower shop. He looked inside and thought, *I should buy some flowers for my wife to take down the aisle*, but then considered *Maybe someone else already has*, and carried on walking.

On their honeymoon in the Bavarian Alps, Lilli's hay fever was so bad that—while all around them young couples stopped to admire gardens bursting with color—they retreated to their hotel room and shut the windows. She sneezed and sneezed until she ended up with one of her recurrent nosebleeds. These could go on for hours. She had an ongoing fear that at some point she would have a nosebleed that simply would not stop, that ribbons of blood would run from her until she lay cold and still. She and Siegfried bonded over their fear of death. In the sink, there grew a pile of crumpled and red-stained handkerchiefs, their own private wildflower display.

Lilli suffered from chest pains and palpitations and, although doctors had reassured them that it was not serious, Siegfried started checking her pulse "almost involuntarily." If they were walking down the street, he held her hand with his forefingers resting on the underside of her wrist, feeling for irregularities.

———

The two of them strolled around the leafy hospital grounds, through the arboretum of exotic pines, sat on a bench to eat their sandwiches. This was his sixth day in hospital and he was relieved to have someone with whom he could speak German. Later that afternoon, he vowed to "get better for my wife."

It was the next afternoon that Siegfried told Dr. Speers that their marriage was "perfect in every respect," this being the kind of phrase to make an analyst reach for their pen. Once Siegfried was given more time to think about it, he acknowledged that there had, after all, been some "periods of concern"—namely Lilli's multiple "unhealthy attachments" to women. These included a relationship with

Siegfried's cousin Elsbeth (a woman to whom Siegfried himself had once proposed), and another one, years later in Turkey, with a fellow German expatriate and close family friend, Gisela Zuckmayer. This latter relationship was so intense that it ended with Lilli "grieving for weeks on end." Siegfried was left to nurse his wife through the heartbreak that resulted from these betrayals, a situation that he did not seem to register as troubling. Lilli's other significant relationship was with Siegfried's own sister Elisabeth—and in this case it had lasted "for a period of years." This relationship, Dr. Speers noted, "was definitely covertly homosexual but apparently not overtly so," a sentence that does not get any clearer with repeat reading.

In light of this information, the fact that Siegfried's hospitalization was triggered by seeing Lilli say goodbye to his sister, watching the two of them embrace on the doorstep, did not seem like mere coincidence.

Over the next two days, Dr. Speers tried to help his patient to comprehend his suppressed negative feelings toward his wife. They discussed how Lilli had been unfaithful several times, in heart and conceivably body, and it was not unreasonable to find this distressing, particularly given his stated attitude to his wife before marriage, that "sexual purity [was] an absolute necessity." But the doctor found him "totally unable to express hostility in any form," except in those rare moments when he was banging his head against a wall. Dr. Speers eventually concluded that "it is useless to attempt to let him understand his hostility . . . [the] patient's insight is lacking and apparently has been all along."

3.

Siegfried woke three times in the night and, on the morning of his tenth day, Dr. Speers found his patient "quite disturbed." He decided to offer a new drug, Marsilid, the first of its kind that did not sedate depressed patients, but left them "energized." Siegfried was given 50 milligrams and by breakfast he was "very pleasant" and "smile[d] a great deal." He ate lunch with enthusiasm, took a further 50 milligrams, then spent some time out in the dayroom "talk[ing] freely to [the] nurse about his life in Germany."

Later in the afternoon, Siegfried spent another two hours with Dr. Speers, who noted his patient's good mood. But although he was "relating well," there was still a deeper resistance—certain things that even chemical assistance could not help Siegfried understand about himself. The doctor believed there could be no further improvements from therapy. Using terms from the new, first edition of the *DSM*—in which homosexuality was listed as a "sociopathic personality disturbance"—he was diagnosed with "anxiety reaction, acute and chronic," and given more of the Marsilid "for elevation of the morning depression," but the basic advice was: stay busy. As if Siegfried didn't already know.

On the morning of Friday, September 20, 1957, Siegfried packed his typewriter into its leather carry case and went around the unit, thanking each nurse in turn. Not once in the many hours he had spent talking about his life had he mentioned chemical weapons.

He was now ready to write his memoirs.

This work began shortly after he left the hospital, finally bringing order to his life by writing it down, placing it all in context with the help of his Brockhaus encyclopedia. Given that his medical notes reveal his most persistent emotions as envy and self-pity, I wondered if his entire memoir was an attempt, whether conscious or not, to build a legacy for himself, ending with the grand performance of his own guilt, the weight of history on his shoulders, when in fact he felt nothing of the sort. Because wasn't there something flattering about the idea of battling for decades with a complex moral burden? Wasn't that preferable to admitting to the pedestrian resentments that, it seemed from his medical records, were the true source of his unhappiness? In which case, I had clearly been duped—as evidenced by the last four years of my life.

He was over a thousand pages in when Lilli died suddenly in the autumn of 1963. She went to bed beside her husband and, while he slept on, her heart stopped—just as Siegfried had always feared it would. She was buried that afternoon in a cemetery off the Durham Road in Chapel Hill and Siegfried soon found himself back in therapy.

This time he visited the private practice of Dr. Marianne Breslin, another German-born psychiatrist. The notes from their sessions have been shredded but—to judge by what he wrote about Lilli's death in his memoir—they would have provided plenty to unpack. The threat of her heart suddenly giving up—"which was seemingly in my subconscious all that time"—had now come true and, as such, he wrote that he felt an uneasy relief because he no longer "lived in constant fear that she would die." Her death made plain the decades he'd spent in anticipation of it. And so, mixed in with the pain of losing Lilli was a sense of release because he now had *less* to live for. This was a unique kind of romance: to love someone so much that you'll never be at ease until they're dead.

The less charitable way of looking at it was arguably more straight-forward. Lilli was the only woman he'd ever kissed, slept beside, or had sex with, and she had spent much of their shared life falling in love with other people. Each time these relationships ended, Siegfried swallowed the betrayal and helped her recover from the pain. Perhaps it was not within his capabilities to see that a part of him might have wanted to be liberated from that situation.

Only after Lilli's death did Siegfried write in his memoirs about what he called her "close relationships with female friends." His theory was that Lilli was drawn to Elisabeth—and to women, in general—because, at age five, she had lost her mother to tuberculosis. While the novels and poetry of the time presented tuberculosis as transformative, almost saintly—its pallid victims ascending into the higher realm with a "hectic glow" at their cheeks—the reality had been less lyrical. Lilli's mother, who had been a successful singer, sweated and spat blood, her lungs filling with mucus, a rotten stench on her breath, while her daughter listened to her coughing through the wall. Given his experience of therapy, perhaps it's unsurprising that Siegfried made sense of Lilli's desire as the transference of un-processed trauma. It may also have been comforting to think that his wife's relationships were not infidelity but grief.

By his own admission, Siegfried was spectacularly, almost proudly, clueless about sexuality, including his own. He claimed that he'd never had a sexual awakening worth the name, nor shared a dirty joke with a schoolmate, nor ever even "imagined engaging in sexual relations with a girl who was not to be my life partner." He was either unusually free of the burden of sexual desire or this was another expression of his talent for self-delusion.

Siegfried had his final session with Dr. Breslin on the same day as President John F. Kennedy's funeral. Jackie Kennedy walked behind her husband's casket and thousands wept in the rain beside the White House. Meanwhile, Siegfried stepped out of the hospital's south wing feeling better than he had in years—and booked no further sessions.

VII.

The Other Side
of the Wall

1.

A month after we'd received the medical notes, my mother and I spent eight nights in an old hotel in Munich, the Marienbad. It had seemed a good idea at the time to book the exact same apartment rooms in which Siegfried and Lilli had spent their wedding night. I don't think we gained much from this immersive research, eating bowls of our own overcooked spätzle while trying not to visualize the newlyweds going at it in the corner. Neither of us slept well that week, which we blamed on the mattresses.

"I'm not sure Opa's going to come across super well," I told my mother as we walked through central Munich. Siegfried had doted on her, his eldest grandchild, and I was worried she might not want to see a less sympathetic version of him in print.

She marched on ahead, counting the door numbers. "Oh well," she said lightly, "you don't write a two-thousand-page memoir if you don't want someone to notice. I think Opa would've just been glad you're interested."

"Not if he could read what I've written," I said.

I followed her past a series of enormous bolted doors. We were looking for the state archives.

"It's fine," my mother said, not breaking stride. "Just say it how you see it."

Beneath an air of approachability—with her open-toed Birkenstocks and tortoiseshell glasses—my seventy-seven-year-old mother was, in the best sense, a cutthroat bastard.

It was some hours later, on Baaderstrasse in the former Jewish district, that my mother bumped into her great-aunt in the street. She noticed a portrait of Elisabeth Merzbacher, Siegfried's older sister, on a poster in a shopwindow, her name in red capitals. We learned that this was part of a campaign to acknowledge the forgotten but groundbreaking women of Munich, a city in which it was easier to find a statue of a horse than of a woman.

The poster featured a short biography of Elisabeth, which my mother translated, accompanied by a QR code, which I pointed my phone at. We read about her moral courage, robust competence, and striking physical beauty: "handsome, balanced features in which there is so much that is serious, difficult and human—and the beautiful blue eyes." As we read further, my mother commented that I had probably been writing about the wrong sibling all along.

2.

We had already been for a look at Siegfried's old boys' school—the Wilhelmsgymnasium, with its corridor of statues, bearded centaurs putting each other in headlocks—so we decided to visit Elisabeth's as well: the School for Higher Daughters. It was now coed and called the Luisengymnasium. We arranged to have a tour and visited on the last day of summer term, when everywhere staff and students greeted each other warmly in the spirit of imminent freedom. Boys and girls played pool together in the common area while, in the staff room, our friendly guide discreetly swept a pile of beer bottle caps into the bin.

We struggled to imagine the atmosphere of suffocating puritanism in which Elisabeth had been schooled. When she was here in the 1890s, morning lessons ended at 11:45 so that the students could be ushered away from the windows before the passing of the noon military parade and the scandalizing gaze of a soldier. She studied sewing for four hours a week and, in the gym, learned to master the gallop, waltz, and swivel hop.

It was only in the school's main hall that my mother and I

glimpsed the old values. There were two historic statues of women in long dresses on either side of the entrance. One was the wise virgin, hand cupped around her oil lamp, guarding her flame from the wind; and the other the foolish virgin, with a tighter dress, her right hand gripping the fabric at her hips and her flame gone out. This being the last day of term, someone had climbed up, and now the wise virgin was wearing lipstick.

After she left school, Elisabeth was expected to be a "house daughter," which essentially meant practicing her domestic skills while waiting for her uncles to choose her a husband. She lived with her parents and siblings in a grand apartment at Residenzstrasse 16, which was already on our list of places we should visit. We walked there to find that the whole building was now a couture menswear and high-end bridal store, four levels of exquisite tweeds and calf leather dress shoes. My mum didn't like the look of it, so I went inside alone.

Apart from the underground parking garage in the middle of the square, the view from the first floor remained largely as it had been a century ago: the palace, the theater, the opera house, a hundred and eighty degrees of unbroken grandeur—wall-to-wall money. I could see my mother on the far pavement, frowning up at the building's buttermilk-colored facade with its six golden gas lamps, ornate ironwork, little stucco dragons holding up a windowsill, all of which I felt was an authentic vision of our family history and she suspected was tacky repro.

When Elisabeth asked to go to university, her parents refused on the grounds that it was unnecessary and unfeminine. Meanwhile, her little brother was already making plans for his further studies, how he would carry the torch for German enlightenment. They had a picture on the wall of Alexander von Humboldt, the famous naturalist and explorer, in whose footsteps her brother was encouraged to follow. They even owned one of Humboldt's rugs, made from the furs and skins of dozens of different animals, rabbit to ermine to fox, all sewn together in concentric circles like a dartboard.

I touched the hem of an unpriced suit jacket made from vicuña, the superfine wool of the wild Andean llama, then went through to the back rooms. Here was a showcase of wedding dresses, floor-to-ceiling mirrors framing mannequins in creaseless silks, chandeliers hanging low above their heads. This was where Elisabeth, against the will of her parents, started her own venture.

Every weekday morning she went down the rear stairs and out into the square, walking south, hurrying past the heavy studded doors of the palace. She met her friend Ida and together they kept going until the streets grew crowded and the hat brims broadened. They reached Gärtnerplatz, where six roads met like the spokes of a wheel. This was where the newcomers settled, *Ostjuden*, Orthodox Jews from the east, many of them refugees who had fled violence in places like Kyiv, Odessa, and Warsaw, only to arrive in a city that did not welcome them, and where they had to look for work in a language they did not speak. Elisabeth and Ida walked past tailors and carpenters, shoemakers and junk shops, back-room synagogues and hawkers selling eggs or fur. They kept their gaze raised, scanning each alleyway. When they heard young people yelling, they walked toward the sound.

By now the local children already recognized Elisabeth—the rich girl with the upright posture and a sweep of golden hair, whose apartment had a phone and an ice cupboard. Their parents had come to trust these young women, not that they had many other options. Even the smallest children roamed the streets unsupervised while the adults tried to make a living. Now the older siblings pushed the younger ones forward.

Some of Munich's middle-class Jews were worried that these "primitive" new arrivals would undo the good work of generations of careful assimilation. People like Elisabeth's father conscientiously donated to respectable refugee charities, avoiding the risk of meeting any actual refugees. He was a board member of one such organization, which reassured its donors that they could help the needy "without fear of social descent or of finding importunate people." Elisabeth took a more hands-on approach.

She and Ida led a chain of six small children beneath the clocktower and back across Marienplatz, heading north. They stopped to watch the sparks spitting from the new overhead tram wires. Eventually they reached Residenzstrasse, taking the rear stairs into the apartment, the clatter of little feet up the lightless spiral, through a dark corridor and into the old playroom. Sitting them on the floor, Elisabeth and Ida took toys down from the high shelves: a bag of marbles; a tray of paper and scissors; a baby doll with lolling eyelids and yellow human hair; and two oval boxes, each containing a tightly packed regiment of tin soldiers—one dressed in blue, one in red. Elisabeth even brought down her expensive dollhouse with its tiny roasting tray in the oven, minute balls of yarn in a knitting bowl, the lady of the house in a rocking chair, linens on her lap. The house that held the life her parents wanted for her. Her future in miniature.

She opened the walls and lifted off the roof.

3.

For the next five years they ran their improvised kindergarten from this room in the family apartment, helped by Elisabeth's younger sister, Luise. It wasn't until April 1904, with financial help from their parents—who had finally come round to the idea—that they rented their own room on Baaderstrasse in the Jewish district. Within months it was clear they needed more space, so they moved down the street, taking two ground-floor rooms, which they also immediately filled. By March 1905, they had moved again into three rooms where, for the first time, their kinder had a garten.

What had begun as an instinctive reaction to seeing very young children on the street was now a registered organization, with space for thirty-five children of all religious backgrounds and a philosophy inspired by the German pedagogue Friedrich Fröbel. Play is "not trivial, but . . . of the deepest meaning," Fröbel wrote, "only this is a free expression of the child's soul." Having spent her own childhood indoors, in a room where her nanny ran a joylessness master class, it felt good to see them all playing together, enjoying the "little garden in the sunshine."

My mother and I tried all the buzzers at Baaderstrasse 5, a bland residential building opposite a parking garage. This was where the kindergarten expanded into a neighboring apartment so that, by 1912, they had the capacity for a hundred young people. Elisabeth was now Elisabeth Kitzinger, married with three children of her own but, supported by her husband, she continued to teach, fundraise, and plan further expansion. The kindergarten started providing after-school care for older kids and, in the evenings, a club where young working women could learn a language, discuss literature, make friends, or—she had not entirely shaken off her father's sense of superiority—learn about "hygiene, which was foreign to them." It was at this point that they put out the word for more volunteers and got a reply from a young woman called Lilli.

Elisabeth and Lilli worked together for two years—as director and volunteer, respectively—and this may have been the start of their "unhealthy attachment." Elisabeth was thirty, married, and pregnant with her fourth child, while Lilli was nineteen, fresh from the same School for Higher Daughters that Elisabeth had attended. In Siegfried's account, Elisabeth "undoubtedly reciprocated" her younger colleague's affection, but Lilli's feelings eventually "became so intense" that Elisabeth was overwhelmed and broke things off. There were—in his words—"scenes." Lilli left the kindergarten, but stayed in touch with Elisabeth—and seven years later she married her brother.

I tried the buzzers at Baaderstrasse 5 again—but no answer.

I had hoped to stand in the garden, thinking I might find the same tree from the one photo of Elisabeth with the children and then, with my eyes closed, let myself be transported—except no

one came to let us in. I tried doing it in the shade of the parking garage, but it wasn't the same. Turning around, I found my mother gone—presumably not keen to watch me visualize a liaison between her grandmother and great-aunt.

"So you think that Lilli was gay?" she asked me when I eventually caught up with her.

"Well . . . I guess it's not completely certain," I said. "She definitely had these relationships with women, but I can't say for sure if they were full-blown affairs or more, you know, deep friendships."

My mother had no interest in believing the most salacious version of the truth. "Probably the latter," she said.

Whatever the reality, the strength of Elisabeth and Lilli's affection for each other was indicated by the fact that there were more letters between them than anyone else among our family's documents. And it was in these letters that Elisabeth wrote to share further developments from the children's home after Lilli had left to become a housewife for her brother. The most significant news came in 1926 when, after decades of renting inadequate facilities, they finally managed to buy somewhere of their own, a beautiful corner building on Antonienstrasse with a garden full of fruit trees and twenty rooms into which the "children moved in beaming." Here they could run a larger kindergarten, after-school clubs, apprenticeships and, for young people with nowhere else to go, offer fifty permanent beds laid with fresh linen.

Hot on the trail, my mother and I bought some pastries then walked to the bus stop.

Antonienstrasse 7 was now a five-story apartment block—potted plants on balconies, a stone Buddha with its back to the street. At first it looked like here, as with the other addresses, no trace of the kindergarten's history remained. But then we noticed that the school across the street was named after Alice Bendix, one of the live-in directors of the children's home. After that we spotted a nearby memorial plaque sticking out of the pavement like a parking meter. It included a 1942 photo of two teenage friends from the home, looking down at the street from a window.

They were laughing.

4.

The first time the authorities tried to shut down the children's home was in the spring of 1933. Elisabeth had good connections at the council's social care department—and knew when to offer a stiff-smiled tour of the building to a pompous councillor, let him make his "tacky little speech." The home reopened after two months, but with reduced funding from the city. When the boiler broke they could not afford to replace it. They eventually got a new one thanks to a large donation from a local woman, non-Jewish, whose generosity was notable because she had to remain anonymous for fear of repercussions.

While Elisabeth was busy trying to fill the growing hole in their finances, the day-to-day running of the home was taken on by a young woman called Alice Bendix. Though Alice could be strict with the children, she had an almost synesthetic understanding of their emotional states. She said she heard the mood of the house as organ music, could sense discord through the floorboards. Her idealism, ambition, and relentless energy could be, to her second-in-command, Hedwig Jacobi, a bit much. Frau Jacobi was older and softer and just a little jaded. She and Elisabeth had worked together for decades and understood each other's tiredness implicitly. But Hedwig and Alice did not need to be friends to make a good team and, under their management, the home flourished, even as the city around them became openly, proudly hostile.

Munich's central synagogue was bulldozed at Hitler's personal request in the summer of 1938. He didn't like its proximity to the Künstlerhaus, a meeting place for the city's artists. By this point, all of Elisabeth's siblings and children had either left the country or were trying to. Her youngest son, who'd moved to London, "pleaded" with his parents to get out. He later told an interviewer: "To me at least it was quite obvious that there was absolutely no future for them." But Elisabeth would not leave her colleagues behind.

The authorities again demanded that the children's home be shut down, and again Elisabeth negotiated an extension. On November 9, 1938, the smaller, Orthodox synagogue—where her father had been chairman and she had spent her childhood—was doused in petrol and set alight, like hundreds of others across the country. Rabbi Ehrentreu tried but failed to save the Torah scrolls and the memorial book of the dead. Firemen did not put out the blaze until noon the next day, by which time the enormous and ornate circular window was a blackened socket.

Elisabeth wrote that a month later "the Nazis had fallen in love with the house on Antonienstrasse" and the harassment had grown personal. She was twice driven out of her apartment. Uniformed men spent a day searching through her belongings. She ended up sleeping in the children's home most nights, sharing the bed of a colleague, Miss Meyer. Elisabeth's husband, Wilhelm, a lawyer, had been arrested and taken to Dachau and she could not bear to be alone at night.

Wilhelm had been summarily imprisoned along with his brother, Rabbi Ehrentreu, and ten thousand other Jewish men from Bavaria and the surrounding regions. Every day Elisabeth and her sister-in-law, Friedel, stood outside the gates at 5 p.m., hoping their partners would be released, feeling the fear compress their chests "like an iron belt." Wilhelm was among the lucky ones, released after a month, stepping through the gate "in a condition that can hardly be described, completely emaciated, of course shaven-headed and dirty, but above all so weak that he could not speak a word." When she arranged for him to have a health check, the "Aryan doctor" said: "I don't know whether I can come to you again because what is today a civic duty is tomorrow a crime."

It was only now that she conceded they needed to leave the country. While her husband recovered at home, she dedicated herself to their emigration—the many forms, stamps, payments, and elaborate bureaucracy—aware that she was just one of countless ghosts gripping their documents on the doorsteps of government offices. By March 1939, they had tickets for a boat to Tel Aviv. At the big house on Antonienstrasse, she said goodbye to the children and their carers. She knew that many of her colleagues had been given opportunities to leave the country. Alice had a brother in Switzerland who was begging her to join him. Hedwig had money and could have tried to pay her way out. They stayed.

From a simple kosher hotel in Tel Aviv, Elisabeth tried to remain present in the daily life of the house on Antonienstrasse. She wrote every week, but always received more mail in return. Alice's many letters suggest that she, like Lilli, had strong feelings for Elisabeth. "Physical separation is only an illusion," she wrote, visualizing herself napping on a sofa in Elisabeth's hotel room or watching Elisabeth cook on her gas stove. She imagined whole conversations between them, tuning into the tone of Elisabeth's voice and "whether there is somewhere a sadness concealed within your words." When Alice was ill, she wrote letters from bed, trying to feel the warmth of Elisabeth's hands. "How much I miss your living, breathing proximity," she wrote. "I have, in all these last years, not found a personal and internal close relationship with anybody apart from yourself and so I emerged from these last couple of days of illness with the awareness that my love would not or could not end in someone else's heart at all, but would just pass through to the beyond." She sent a copy of Rilke's letters to Tel Aviv so that at night they could read from the same book.

Over the next two years, the letters from Alice grew steadily shorter and the paper on which they were written thinned into transparency. The first deportations happened on November 20, 1941. Late at night a bus pulled into the yard of Antonienstrasse. Twenty-three young children—ages between one and eight—were taken to Milbertshofen Station, where they were lifted onto railroad cars. The train was so overcrowded that luggage had to be tossed out and left on the platform, a tacit acknowledgment of what was to come. For three days they traveled north before reaching Kovno (now Kaunas) in Lithuania. They were among almost a thousand Munich Jews who were walked to a fort in which pits had already been dug. They were locked up and starved for two days, then shot in rows of fifty, their bodies burned and buried. In Munich's official documents the missing were noted as having "emigrated to unknown."

In March of the following year, a group of older children, ages between eight and fifteen—along with several employees from the children's home—were transported to Piaski in Poland, a town that was used as a short-term stop on the way to the extermination camps. Their dates and places of death remain unknown.

Alice, Hedwig, and the last thirteen children were taken away in a furniture van. The building on Antonienstrasse now changed from a children's home into a "mothers' home," having been requisitioned as part of the Nazis' Lebensborn program to increase the numbers of "racially pure" children. Here, unmarried mothers of a suitable heritage were encouraged to carry to term pregnancies they might otherwise have terminated.

Alice and Hedwig did their best to make the children comfortable at Milbertshofen, a cramped transit camp, where they all shared one room in a former barracks. The diary of fifteen-year-old Esther Cohn described the space as "being beautifully decorated" and noted that Miss Bendix found her a good mattress so that "I don't feel anything from the hard bed." But they could not prevent some of the children from hearing the "indescribable, hopeless screaming" of fellow prisoners tortured and locked in the boiler house.

By the summer of 1942, they had one fewer child in their care after Esther Cohn volunteered to move to what the SS called the "spa town" of Theresienstadt. From there, she was later transferred to Auschwitz. Meanwhile, Alice and Hedwig and the remaining children were moved to a requisitioned Catholic monastery on the outskirts of Munich. Elisabeth received a final letter from Alice, though it came via the Red Cross and was closer to a telegram, twenty-five words or less and required to be "strictly personal." "Better accommodation since July, monastery building, health good . . . Always thinking of you with love and warmest wishes, Alice."

5.

My mother and I caught the train out to Berg am Laim, a residential suburb in the east of the city. After crossing the highway we walked until the traffic noise grew quiet, then we peeled off into woodland. The church was still there, but the monastery had been replaced by a home for "assisted living"—low-rise apartments that looked out on a pretty lawn with a birdbath and sundial.

In 1942, the nuns had tried to make life bearable for the Jewish children who were brought here. They played games with them in the garden and the observant were invited to make use of the church. On Friday nights they celebrated the Sabbath in the rococo chapel among a kaleidoscope of glimmer and gold. Above the doorway to the church—then, as now—there was a statue of Archangel Michael, his crown glowing as he drove a spear through the devil's neck.

On March 12, 1943, Alice and Hedwig were given twenty-four hours' notice. They had time to cut the children's hair. As the final hour approached, the children seemed "calm and collected and of an almost cheerful, optimistic disposition." On a passenger train, Alice, Hedwig, and the remaining children traveled to Auschwitz, where, according to a witness, they were selected on arrival and taken by truck to Birkenau to be "disinfected." After undressing they were locked inside a room with showerheads on the walls. The lights went off. Pellets dropped in through overhead shafts. The children were the first to die as the hydrocyanic gas, heavier than air, filled the room from the bottom up. Afterward, the Jewish camp prisoners who were forced to pull apart the corpses wore gas masks with a "J" filter. This was among the masks produced by Siegfried's former department in Oranienburg—the protection division.

6.

Elisabeth no longer wanted to go outside. She was seventy years old and living in Washington, DC, in the home of her son, Ernst. Outwardly she looked elegant and upright—her silver hair now so fine as to be semitransparent—but her agoraphobia and arthritis had worsened to the point where she rarely left the house. Her rooms were kept like an outpost of turn-of-the-century Bavaria, full of cigarette smoke and the heavy Biedermeier furniture that had somehow traveled with her from Munich via Tel Aviv. Once a week her son and his wife, a Gentile whom Elisabeth treated with a subtle but persistent hostility, came to eat the heavy German stews she cooked in her own small kitchen. They walked across the landing with a feeling of crossing continents.

She was loved by her grandchildren, though she could be intimidating. In her granddaughter's recollection, she wore only black, never laughed, and "did not speak about the past ever ever ever." Three evers. "The overwhelming feeling was of silence imposed over so much." Her letters reveal her efforts to teach her grandkids to speak German. She felt they lacked the necessary resilience, noting that her grandson was unable "to hide it when he was suffering. Children brought up in the modern way don't do that, anyway."

After the last message from her colleagues at Antonienstrasse in August 1942, it was rumored that they were alive and confined to Theresienstadt, and Elisabeth spent those years waiting and hoping for news that never came. In 1943 her daughter, Gretel, had surgery in Haifa and died on the operating table. In 1944 her husband died of a heart attack in Tel Aviv, having never fully recovered from his time in Dachau. She moved to America in 1947 and kept willfully busy. Sitting out on the freezing-cold porch, she made pocket money mending oriental rugs from the homes of rich congressmen and academics, surrounded by her hooked needles and a stack of patches and fabrics, her agile hands in constant movement.

She never took to life in America, even as her younger sister showed her what was possible. Each day, Luise walked miles through the suburbs, going door-to-door with her satchel of Avon cosmetics and her strong German accent, hand-selling creams to housewives, perfuming fifty wrists a day. Then she came home and played Scrabble with her sister, the "shut-in," at the ornate Biedermeier table.

By the late 1950s—just as her brother began writing his memoir in which Elisabeth's forty-year career was summarized in two breezy paragraphs—a handful of people started taking an interest in Elisabeth's former work in Munich. There were two academic articles, and her eightieth birthday was celebrated by Rabbi Baerwald in the *Aufbau* magazine, who wrote that she "has proved that the energy of a real person often achieves more than large organizations." He acknowledged the pain of having seen "her beautiful work destroyed," but hoped she would "look back with satisfaction on hundreds of children and young people who . . . have her to thank for leading normal and useful lives."

Meanwhile, she was entirely reliant on the care of others. She had developed shin splints so that, along with her other health issues, she now limped and required the support of her forgiving daughter-in-law. By early 1965, her care needs had gone beyond what her family could provide and she was transferred to a hospice on Wisconsin Avenue, a place with a name well suited to someone who did not believe in pity: Washington Home for Incurables.

A few months later, her brother moved to Washington so that, for the first time since their childhoods in Munich, the three siblings were living in the same city. Each had outlived their spouse. Siegfried and Luise rented rooms in the Roosevelt Hotel, which had once been a high-society hot spot with a ballroom, a marble-columned lobby, and a basement nightclub where you could listen to Benny Goodman or the Glenn Miller Orchestra while white-gloved waiters brought out oysters and chateaubriand. That was before it was shut down due to bad plumbing and reopened as the Roosevelt Hotel for Senior Citizens, a four-hundred-room facility that advertised itself as somewhere "to escape the noise and confusion of the business district." The three siblings saw each other every day, either at the hospice or, if Elisabeth was feeling mobile, on the eighth floor of the Roosevelt with a skyline view. They kept up their daily game of Scrabble, alternating English and German.

Now eighty-four, Elisabeth had only ever produced one short and stiffly factual account of her work life. She had no interest in writing a memoir and yet—seeing her brother hammering away at his version of events, closing in on half a million words—her memories nagged at her. Her mind returned to the women she'd worked with in Munich, many of whom had the chance to escape but chose not to.

At the hospice, Elisabeth went to her boxes of correspondence and laid out all the letters on the bed. She decided to write about her colleagues: a handful of one-page biographies, simple and unsentimental, recording lives that had seemed to vanish without trace. The problem was that—while she had many personal messages from these women, letters in which they described their dreams, favorite poems, least favorite coworkers, the lilacs blooming in the Englischer Garten, or the bout of flu that took out the entire Tuesday night sewing group—she was missing several essential facts. In particular, she could not say for sure when they were born or when they died. So she set about writing to their relatives, the sound of her typing now matching her brother's in his room across town. While he described his daily experiments to measure how long Auer's specialized filters could hold out against hydrogen cyanide in an enclosed space, she wrote that her young protégé, Alice, was deported to Auschwitz—"presumably."

Elisabeth made slow progress and was still trying to pin down the facts as her health rapidly declined. She developed diabetes, her limbs swelling up until she was unable to leave her room. There her condition worsened, eventually requiring the amputation of her left leg.

By August 1965, typing from bed, she had finally gathered enough information to write a few hundred words each about her former colleagues, although, "despite all my efforts," some exact birth dates still eluded her. She sent her pages to London, to a publisher that had put out a call for contributions to a book memorializing those who had given their lives to help others.

It took me some time to track down a copy of the book, *Preservation in Decline*, published in 1965. It was forbiddingly austere, the editors noting that "it did not seem appropriate to us, given the terrible seriousness of this documentation of the lost, to measure the portrayal by literary or artistic standards." The book was long out of print and last borrowed from the library in 1984—and Elisabeth's biographies were not in it. They had arrived in London shortly after the book had gone to print. She wrote to ask if her colleagues might be included in any subsequent editions, but there weren't any.

Mr. Elisabeth Kitzinger, Washington 18.8.1965.

ALICE BENDIX.

Alice Bendix, geboren um 1895 in Koenigsberg, hat bis zum Juli 1933 als Jugendleiterin im Charlottenburger Jugendheim , Berlin gearbeitet. Dort wurde ihr dank ihrer Tuechtigkeit manche schwierige Aufgabe uebertragen.

1933 kam Alice Bendix nach Muenchen, und uebernahm die Leitung des Kinderheims der Israelitischen Jugendhilfe E.V. Ihr hervorragendes Organisationstalent, ihr tiefes Verstaendnis fuer jedes einzelne Kind und fuer jede einzelne Mitarbeiterin waren von groesstem Wert in jenen schweren Jahren. Auch verstand sie den Kontakt mit den Eltern trotz aller Schwierigkeiten aufrecht zu erhalten. Sie selbst stellte sich nie in den Vordergrund, hatte aber die Zuegel immer fest in der Hand. Eine grosse Stuetze war sie den jungen Maedchen, die im Heim in Kinderpflege und Haushalt ausgebildet wurden, als Vorbereitung fuer die Auswanderung.

Im Jahre 1942 wurde das Heim, in dem damals noch 12 Kinder waren, von den Nazis aufgeloest, und in in einem kleinen Kloster in Berg am Laim bei Muenchen untergebracht. Gemeinsam mit Hedwig Jacobi schuf Alice Bendix dort eine letzte Heimstaette fuer die 12 verbliebenen Kinder. Nach dem Bericht einer frueheren arischen Mitarbeiterin, die den Mut hatte, dieses " Kinderheim" bis zur Deportation regelmaessig zu besuchen, herrschte dort trotz aller Primitivitaet eine gemuetliche friedliche Atmosphaere.

Im Maerz 1943 wurde Alice Bendix mit den Kindern vermutlich nach Auschwitz deportiert und fand dort ihren Tod.

ALICE BENDIX, born around 1895 in Königsberg, [born November 13, 1894, in Landsberg an der Warthe] was a youth care worker in the Charlottenburg orphanage in Berlin until July 1933. Because she was extremely skilled and productive, she was given a lot of responsibility during her time there, including many difficult tasks.

In 1933, Alice Bendix came to Munich and took over the leadership of the Jewish Youth Aid's orphanage. Her outstanding organizational talent, her deep understanding of each individual child and employee were of great value during those difficult years. She also succeeded in maintaining contact with the parents despite all the difficulties. She never drew attention to herself, while always holding the reins firmly. She was a great support to the young girls who were trained in child-rearing and housekeeping in preparation for emigration.

In 1942, the home was closed down by the Nazis and transferred to a small monastery in Berg am Laim near Munich. Together with Hedwig Jacobi, Alice Bendix created a final home for the remaining twelve children. According to a former Aryan employee who had the courage to visit regularly until the deportation, a cozy, peaceful atmosphere prevailed, despite the comparatively primitive premises. In March 1943, Alice Bendix was deported with the children, presumably to Auschwitz, where she met her death.

Mrs Elisabeth Kitzinger, Washington 18·8·1965?

HEDWIG JACOBI.

Hedwig Jacobi, geboren 1879 in Wuerzburg, arbeitete in jungen Jahren zunaechst als freiwillige Helferin im Kinderhort der Israelitischen Jugendhilfe in Muenchen. Zu Beginn des 1. Weltkrieges uebernahm sie gemeinsam mit ihrer Freundin Marta Reutlinger, gestorben 1938, die Leitung des ganzen Betriebes., Kindergarten und Hort. Grosse Aufgaben mussten erfuellt werden. So musste z.B. in den ungenuegenden Raeumen eine Kinderspeisung fuer 150 Kinder eingerichtet werden. Hedwig Jacobi hat mit ihrem praktischen Sinn, mit ihrem Organisationstalent und ihrer Energie es verstanden, allen Anforderungen gerecht zu werden. So hat sie die Zubereitung der Mahlzeiten freiwilligen Helferinnen - besonders tuechtigen Hausfrauen uebergeben. Dabei hatte sie selbst immer die Zuegel fest in der Hand und half aus, wo es noetig war.

Nach dem 1. Weltkrieg war es dringend noetig, Kinder intern aufzunehmen. Im Jahre 1926 gelang es der Israelitischen Jugendhilfe E.V. ein schoenes Haus mit Garten zu erwerben, Dort fanden 30 Kinder ihr Heim und 45 junge Maedchen wurden in Kinderpflege und Haushalt ausgebildet, von 1933 an als Vorbereitung zur Auswanderung. Hedwig Jacobi, die nunmehr wieder ehrenamtlich arbeitete, hat in diesen Jahren dank ihrer Tuechtigkeit und Hingabe viel zum Erfolg der Arbeit beigetragen. Sie blieb dem Kinderheim treu bis in den Tod.

Im Jahre 1942, als das Kinderheim von den Nazis aufgeloest wurde, und die verbliebenen 12 Kinder in einem Kloster in der Naehe von Muenchen untergebracht wurden, folgte auch Hedwig Jacobi ihnen dorthin. Gemeinsam mit Alice Bendix schuf sie dort eine letzte Haimstaette fuer die Kinder, und gemeinsam mit ihnen wurde sie im Maerz 1943 von dort vermutlich nach Auschwitz deportiert.

HEDWIG JACOBI, born [November 16] 1879 in Würzburg, worked for the Jewish Youth Aid in Munich during her youth—as a volunteer at first. At the beginning of the First World War, she took on, together with her friend Marta Reutlinger (d. 1938), the management of the whole organization, kindergarten, and after-school care. There were big tasks to be fulfilled. Thus, for example, it was necessary to arrange a canteen for 150 children in the inadequate rooms. Hedwig Jacobi managed to fulfill all demands due to her practical sense, her organizational skills, and her energy. For example, she delegated the preparation of meals to volunteers—especially proficient housewives. During the process, she always firmly held the reins and helped where necessary.

After the First World War, it was urgently necessary to accept more children into the home. In 1926, the Jewish Youth Aid succeeded in buying a beautiful house with a garden. There, thirty children found their home and, from 1933, forty-five young girls were educated in child-rearing and household skills in preparation to emigrate. Hedwig Jacobi, who was now working voluntarily again, contributed a lot to the home's success, thanks to her proficiency and devotion. She stayed faithful to the orphanage until her death.

In 1942, when the home was disbanded by the Nazis and the remaining twelve children were provided with accommodation in a monastery close to Munich, Hedwig Jacobi followed them there. Together with Alice Bendix she created a final home for the children and was, together with them, most likely deported to Auschwitz in March 1943.

7.

Construction began on a new synagogue for Munich in 2003. Even before the cornerstone was laid, authorities uncovered plans to blow it up. Members of a neo-Nazi group called the Kameradschaft Süd (Southern Fellowship) were arrested after police raided a Munich apartment and found grenades, guns, a double-headed axe, various swastika pennants, and 1.7 kilograms of TNT.

The synagogue was inaugurated on November 9, 2006—sixty-eight years to the day after the old Orthodox one was burned down. My mother and I were guided through security by Ellen Presser, the head of the Cultural Center of the Jewish Community of Munich. She explained that Munich's liberal Jewish community was growing again, led by an atmosphere of increased openness and a female cantor. She contrasted this with the falling membership of the Berlin congregation, who were under the leadership of, as she put it, "the Jewish Boris Johnson."

Here in Munich, the community center hosted film nights and soccer team socials, a kosher restaurant, a primary school, and a kindergarten that, like Elisabeth's, welcomed Jewish and non-Jewish children. As we continued our tour, Ellen and my mother kept chatting in German, despite my complaints, perhaps because they knew that this was a good way to avoid being included in my book. When I asked them to translate what they were discussing, Ellen warmly reprimanded me for not speaking good enough German and then reprimanded my mother for not teaching me.

We followed her through wood-paneled corridors and offices as she plucked books of history from shelves and piled them in my arms. Ellen's own parents were Holocaust survivors from what is now Poland and Ukraine, and she remained stateless for most of her life. This had nothing to do with bureaucracy. Although she was born in Munich she chose not to be German. This decision reflected not just her relationship to Germany but to statehood in general. She had no faith that a passport—any passport—would protect her when it really mattered. Her parents had both been Polish citizens but their nationality had done nothing to save them from the Nazis. Ellen was fifty-two when, in 2006, she finally became German—in the same year the new Munich synagogue opened. Not that she mentioned any of this while we were with her, walking through a large hall that smelled of tomato sauce. I noticed a single swirl of fusilli wedged beneath the leg of one of the rows of foldout tables. Hundreds of Ukrainian Jews had recently arrived in Munich, fleeing the war. They were staying in the city in B and Bs where they were not allowed to cook their own meals, so twice a day, every day, they came here to eat.

A few months after my mother and I returned home, we heard that some of the remains of the original Munich central synagogue, knocked down in June 1938 at Hitler's request, had been rediscovered. Workmen doing maintenance on a weir on the Isar noticed that the rubble buried in the riverbed was unusually ornate. The great chamber of worship with its three octagonal turrets had been used as filler. Now eighty-five years later, the workmen pulled it from the river.

VIII.
Naturalizing

1.

My mother had been given a date for our final meeting at the embassy in London. We would soon be German, regardless of what we had learned in our research. Meanwhile, my cousin had brought me a box file of letters in which Siegfried found God in the summer of 1965. Exactly half a century after he had abandoned his father's piousness in a restaurant in Hamburg, he had an epiphany in room 822 at the Roosevelt Hotel for Senior Citizens.

His older sister, Elisabeth, had just moved to the Home for Incurables and he was reading a nonfiction book called *Virus*. It described the extraordinary power of infections as they spread, each bacterial cell dividing into its daughter cells, gaining speed and lethality until it reaches millions of organisms in an "avalanche of reproduction." The book questioned the boundary between the dead and the living because, in the right conditions, viruses are essentially immortal. It noted that the word "virus" came from the Latin meaning "poison." After reading it, Siegfried wrote that the "amazing research results of modern science reveal the work of a divine being. I can't understand how so many people ignore this and still complain that there is no revelation these days."

The book itself was essentially atheistic, arguing that the miraculous virulence of a disease like typhus was proof that, in order to believe in God, you would have to concede his absolute indifference to humans—which is precisely what Siegfried took from it. "So I'm a believer," he wrote, though "of course, I cannot believe in a benevolent, anthropomorphic God, the Father in Heaven. . . . I also can't believe in a personal life after death and in a reunion with loved ones." No, for him "God is far too sublime to care about every living being. . . . We, as small, insignificant humans, must humbly submit to this higher law. . . . I can't pray. I cannot expect God to take care of the worries and needs of a tiny earthworm"—by which he meant himself. Here was a faith that meant he was of no more or less value than the unicellular organisms reproducing themselves in the dirt—and this was clearly a relief. And though he did not say as much, one could see how this revelation would also suit a man with his professional history. He would not be judged by a God who took no special interest in human life.

The other notable thing about Siegfried's religious transformation was the person he chose to share it with. That was one Frau Rose Quasebart—the wife of his old boss in Oranienburg. They had last met in person in 1935, when she and Lilli—both married to chemical weapons specialists working for the Nazis—hit it off instantly, finding "much in common." Rose immigrated to Switzerland in 1943, leaving her husband behind. After his death, she never remarried. Now, decades later, she had spotted Siegfried's name in a Swiss magazine, *Die Weltwoche*, and started up a correspondence. Siegfried and Rose wondered if they might not be too old to meet up in the flesh. "Your letters are so beautiful," Siegfried told her. "You are the only person with whom I can speak openly about these things."

Rose Quasebart had noticed Siegfried's name in the magazine's letters section. This, it turned out, was just one of many letters that Siegfried had written to various publications. Simultaneous with his work on the memoir, he had been undertaking a concerted one-man campaign in support of worldwide demilitarization and disarmament. Writing to the *Aufbau*, the *Charlotte Observer*, and repeatedly to the *New York Times*, he acknowledged that while, in the age of the atom bomb, civilian bunkers were a necessity beneath every home, they would only encourage "war psychosis" if not accompanied by open de-escalation. He was writing this, he said, as someone with senior experience of "the protection of the civilian population against warfare agents." In one letter, he specified which filter, make and model, would best neutralize radioactive particulates. The responses were predictable. "Your letter has been noted by the editorial staff. . . . We regret that we are not able to publish it."

Eventually he tried writing directly to the White House:

Dear Mr. President . . . I propose that all forces, which have hitherto been employed directly or indirectly by the military, be utilized in a number of large scale international cooperative scientific, technical and economic ventures: the exploration of space and of the oceans as well as the interior of the earth, the lifting of the standard of living of underdeveloped nations. . . . Bold and utopian as my proposals must seem, this is a time in which strong and radical ideas are needed if we are not to slide from the cold into the hot war almost inadvertently. . . .

At first it seemed contradictory to me that Siegfried wrote these idealistic letters while simultaneously minimizing his own collaboration with the military. But perhaps both projects were an expression of the same thing. In his letters he envisioned a safer future and in his memoirs he invented a safer past. Two days after he sent his proposals for world peace to the White House, the Russians began building a wall through the center of Berlin: twenty-seven miles protected with barbed wire, attack dogs, and land mines.

2.

After Elisabeth's death in 1966, Siegfried and Luise moved together to German-speaking London—a neighborhood where the bus conductors announced the stop as "Finchleystrasse," sometimes adding "Have your passports ready please." Here there were cafés serving sauerbraten and strudel and the local supermarket stocked tinned blutwurst and brined white asparagus. The two siblings found rooms in a German-Jewish care home.

My mother and I visited Finchley Road together and stood outside Ye Olde Swiss Cottage, a faux-Alpine party pub stranded in six lanes of traffic, trying to believe it was in some way historical. My mother had been twenty-two when she used to visit her Opa every week, even getting to know the other residents in the home, mostly former refugees whose lives of extraordinary upheaval did not stop her finding "some of them extremely boring."

We headed down the steep hill to Siegfried's old address, Greencroft Gardens. My mother remembered how he had made a ritual of his visits to the non-kosher butchers, the walk uphill with his cane, the hand-cranked meat slicer, a few pink slivers of ham in a greaseproof sheet, sneaking them back to his room in a suit pocket. The God he now believed in couldn't care less. At number 69, we peered in through the ground-floor window, the glass half-misted for privacy. On my phone we looked at pictures of Siegfried in this room, age eighty-five and still working on his memoirs at his typewriter. He was wearing a black suit and tie as though ready, at any moment, for a funeral.

My dad used to join my mother on her visits, and in his memory of it, they always ate the same meal in the home's dining room: ox tongue and capers. This was before my parents got married. My father was proving his commitment by making small talk with his girlfriend's strange, carefree grandpa in a house that smelled of boiling tongues.

It speaks to a paucity of other research materials that I thought it worthwhile to cook an ox tongue, just to get a sense of it. The butcher gave me what looked like a sodden dishcloth. At home I held it, dripping, then plunged it into a pot of boiling water, where it instantly came alive. As it writhed and flexed, I tried to push it under with a wooden spoon, but it would not stay down. It kept lifting the lid off the pot.

Siegfried died painlessly at breakfast time on April 3, 1971. He had been staying with my grandmother in Edinburgh. My aunt remembered him from this time as just "sitting, watching the world go on around him. He was a really peaceful, benign presence." He was also eighty-eight and suffering from carcinoma of the bladder. For a man who had spent much of his life anticipating his own death, nobody paid much attention when it finally happened. My mum had to speak to the registry office to check she had the date right. As usual she got on well with the lady behind the desk so that even when Siegfried Merzbacher's name could not be found on the records, the clerk persevered. They eventually found him under a misspelling.

About the ceremony at the crematorium, my relatives remembered nothing. I found a copy of the eulogy, written and delivered by an unknown family member. It described how—right up until his death—Siegfried still talked about needing to finish his memoirs.

In the 400 degree Celsius furnace, his body would have quickly adopted the "pugilistic attitude," hunched over in the manner of a boxer, shoulders raised and fists clenched as the flexor muscles contracted. (Firefighters are taught not to mistake this stance for a "pre-death attempt to shield oneself from an attacker.") His body cavities would have become visible after thirty minutes. Complete incineration would have taken two or three hours, sending carbon dioxide, particulates, and heavy metals into the Edinburgh sky. A recent study found high levels of mercury in the hair of crematoria staff—due to the element being released during the burning of dental amalgam. But if Siegfried had his dentures in—made of acrylic—they would have burned quite clean.

3.

Our citizenship certificates, embossed with gold, were fanned out on the coffee table in an office of the German embassy in London. Juliane, our friendly guide through this process, explained that we would not actually *become* German citizens until the moment we physically picked up these documents—and she wanted us to know that it was not too late to change our minds. She said we should feel free to realize, even at this stage, that we were making a big mistake. My parents, one of my sisters, and I, sitting on chairs in a quarter circle, all looked down at the certificates, each of which came with a pin badge showing both British and German flags plus a complimentary pack of vegan Haribo gummy bears, cruelty-free, made in Bonn.

Juliane seemed to know more about our family history than we did. She talked us through the cold bureaucracy that lay behind our family's statelessness, how it had all happened in government buildings like this one and, in a sense, she said, "by people like me." Herr Heller of the Potsdam secret police had canceled my grandmother Dorothea's citizenship with a flick of his pen, a decision that five years later led her to seek refuge in marriage with my British grandfather, a relationship that quickly produced my mother, who was now the first of us to pick up her documents—and turn German.

Juliane smiled and asked, "How do you feel?"

My mother weighed the papers in her hand. "*In*teresting," she said.

I picked up the documents on behalf of my children, turning my son German during his school lunch hour, my daughter waking German from her nap. Then my sister and I picked up our papers, too, and my mother was right. It was interesting, simultaneously fraudulent and profound. While no burdens were suddenly lifted, there was a flash of connectedness, a sense of generations spreading out behind and ahead of us, like when you pull apart a paper chain and suddenly see all the human-shaped figures, dangling and holding on to each other. But on the other hand, there was the undeniable sense that the whole thing was a long con to get our EU passports back after Brexit. It felt deeply meaningful and completely dishonest at exactly the same time.

Perhaps sensing our uncertainty, Juliane asked what my grandmother would have thought about us becoming German, to which my mother replied flatly: "She wouldn't have liked it." Juliane looked pleased at this answer, perhaps because—in acknowledging that our becoming German was problematic—my mother was being distinctly German.

Afterward, we put on our pin badges and stepped out into Belgravia's embassyland with its atmosphere of hidden assets. There was Bahrain, Brunei, Luxembourg, Malaysia, a different flag in every doorway. We had hoped to mark this day with a traditional

German lunch, but could only find an international food hall near Victoria station and none of the stalls were German.

Over gyoza and fried chicken, we asked our mother why she thought Granny would not have approved. She said she was thinking of how, at twenty-one, Dorothea had left behind her family and friends, abandoned her studies, and swapped everything for a British passport that would improve the lives of her children and her children's children, who—look at us now—were chomping down on the gummy bears of our murderous nationhood.

She may not have phrased it exactly like that. I felt differently, though. At the other end of Dorothea's life, when dementia and depression were closing in, when she disliked pretty much everything—including but not limited to underfloor heating, food, and people walking with objects in their hands—her only real source of excitement was speaking German with her new eighty-five-year-old boyfriend, Ernst. Every time the phone rang, her eyes opened wide—"Oh, that'll be my man"—and she would disappear into her bedroom. I remember the sound of her voice, suddenly bright and warm, speaking German through the wall.

At home, I found Ernst's number in an old address book and decided to cold-call. My grandmother had met him at a mutual friend's funeral, an instant connection among the headstones. He was a retired architect living alone in Greenock, a small town on the Clyde. They were both widowed and glad to find someone with whom they could speak the language of their childhoods, chatting for hours like teenagers. And while she was increasingly rude to her closest family, she saved her good humor for him.

He picked up on the thirteenth ring.

"This is the grandson of Dorothea Brander," I said. "I don't know if you remember her?"

It had been six years since she died.

"Oh yes, God, dear God, I remember her." He paused for a moment. "She still lives with me."

And then we were off. We talked for over an hour, the conversation only interrupted when he smelled burning from the kitchen—his corn on the cob boiling dry. I called him every day that week and started to understand why my grandmother had fallen for him, his crackly, slow voice at the end of a phone line, and the way he pronounced her name with a hard *th*. His background was not Jewish, he explained. He had grown up in a Christian family, who remained in Germany throughout "those godless years." And yet he and Dorothea had a profound connection, partly because they were both Germans living in Britain. On that subject, Ernst believed that the Brexit vote, the severing of the union, had damaged him at a physical level, causing a rupture inside him from which his digestive system had never recovered, and then we chatted for a while about laxatives.

We also talked through the story of my grandmother's life, about which he remembered everything, adding details that were new to me. According to Ernst there had been someone *before* my grandfather, some formative relationship in Turkey in 1942, when she was eighteen—but, despite my efforts, Ernst honorably maintained her confidence. He said only that she had experienced "a private release of all these incredible tensions."

I fact-checked this with my mother, who was, fortunately, less discreet. She had come across letters to this man, a German called Georg, when clearing out my grandmother's apartment after her death. My mother's opinion was that Dorothea had been much more in love with Georg than he was with her, and that she kept writing him love letters despite his disinterest. When I asked to see the correspondence, my mother explained with no remorse that she had thrown everything in the bin, "so, from your point of view, he doesn't exist." According to my sister, our grandfather Donald also had a long-running affair with a Scottish painter. After his death, Dorothea still kept one of the other woman's gloomy abstract paintings on the wall because, as my grandmother said, "She was a very good artist."

Ernst also knew the story of how my grandparents met. Dorothea was nineteen, stateless, and Donald was thirty-six, her English tutor and a British citizen. Donald told her that, back in Scotland, he was a lecturer at Glasgow University and that he came from a distinguished farming family on the Isle of Arran. She only learned the truth after they were married and arriving in northeast Glasgow to meet his parents and three sisters in a pebbledash council block, his father's accent so thick that she couldn't understand a word. It was, by this point, too late to change her mind. She was thousands of miles away from her family and already pregnant with my mother. And yet, somehow, this marriage built on passports and deceit worked out well.

On the fifth day of interviewing Ernst—which mostly involved listening as his thoughtful sentences flowed on, seamlessly, one into another, ranging across decades and continents—a memory returned to me of seeing my grandmother on the phone with him, rolling her eyes and holding the handset away from her ear. Yadda-yadda-yadda. She had a finite interest in the past even when—especially when——it was her own. I had liked the idea that her getting a German boyfriend was a symbolic counterpart to our German passports, but I was increasingly aware that this was precisely the kind of self-serving notion that she would have enjoyed shooting down.

During my final call with Ernst, he said: "I have to tell you I loved your grandmother. . . . I loved her for her Germanness. She couldn't help it." They could say things to each other they would not say to anyone else, he explained. I thought of Siegfried's profound connection with Frau Quasebart and the power of a relationship in which no subject is off-limits. "I found somebody to whom I could speak openly and she spoke openly to me," Ernst said, and then, not for the first time, his breathing grew heavy on the line. "For me, there are no more awkward questions," he said. "I have found, if not peace, then the basis on which my realities are assembled."

In the last few months of her life, my grandmother started saying that she and Ernst were going to drive down to Marseille together and see the Mediterranean. Considering that she hadn't left Edinburgh in over a year, that she'd long ago become a significant risk to other road users and we'd taken away her car keys, this was quite a plan. But the carers advised us not to contradict her. At this point, they said, facts ceased to matter. So we went with the story she wanted to believe in, watched her pack a small suitcase to keep by the door. We agreed that she would soon be at the wheel, steering them south, her architect boyfriend reclining beside her as they blazed down a road carved into the mountainside. With their windows open, they would take the long route, a river coiled beneath them, their eyes blasted wide by the wind.

4.

I returned all my documents to the bottom drawer labeled *family archive*, putting back far more than I had taken out. I was contributing fifty pages of Freudian analysis from a psychiatric unit in North Carolina, Elisabeth's biographies of her colleagues from the children's home, a wide range of letters my mother had translated, documents concerning the Turkish government's purchase of chemical weapons in 1937, and a lump of bleached rubble from Ammendorf. Nobody thanked me. I'd also had Siegfried's memoir rebound, after it finally fell apart from overuse. I was still wearing the ring my mother had given me for my wedding, the oval bloodstone, black with flecks of red. I wondered what I would say if I ever passed it on to my children or grandchildren. Fortunately, my now six-year-old son had already made it absolutely clear that he would never get married or reproduce.

At home my Geiger counter was buried in the drawer I reserve for things I hope never to see again. But in the autumn of 2023, my wife started work as a gardener at a park that I remembered— from my time on the spectrometry forums—was the site of illegally dumped radioactive waste. That was London's Olympic Park, just down the road from where we live. Every morning she cycled there in a high-visibility safety vest to spend her days in the soil.

I arranged to meet a man with a backpack full of documents he'd uncovered by Freedom of Information request. He chose a place called Café Z. His papers included "Radiation & Contamination Survey Reports" of the then-prospective Olympic site from 2008 by a company called Nukem. The former brownfield site had a long history of heavy industry. During the clearance, the construction team discovered around a hundred tons of radioactive waste that, legally, should have been disposed of by meticulous and expensive specialists. Instead—as the park was being readied for the Olympics and under the lax mayoral guidance of Boris Johnson—the contractors found a work-around. They mixed the radioactive material with a far larger volume of ordinary, nonradioactive waste, so that the overall radioactivity of the pile dropped to an acceptable level. They then buried the lot in an enormous concrete tomb that became part of the landscaping of the park, a short sprint from where the world's best athletes then ran loops at extraordinary speed, many of whom were later found to be drugged to the eyeballs, so that London's Olympics smashed the world record for the greatest number of doping violations. At the time the radioactive waste was discovered, only the *Guardian* showed interest in the story, and this minor scandal was quickly buried beneath the festivities of the Olympic fortnight. Not that I can claim any moral high ground. I was among the thousands at the basketball arena, clapping and laughing when the mayor came on court to do a funny dance. But after the tourists and athletes went home, the concrete chamber of variably radioactive waste was still there, near where my wife now sat each day to eat her sandwiches.

An expert report from 2009 concluded that there was "significant contamination of the site with uranium, radium and thorium isotopes," the half-lives of which, in some cases, were more than a thousand years. Among the recommendations was that "people working at the site and those living downwind of the dusts generated at the site have a flag to this effect placed on their medical records." When she came back from work, I showed this to my wife. We had been living a mile from the Olympic Park throughout the years of construction.

I put fresh batteries in the Geiger counter and my son and I cycled out to where the coffin—"the disposal cell"—had been buried, built into the base of one of the bridges and next to the wetlands. We started hunting for the "hottest" locations. I dug a little hole in the soil beside one of the trees. Radiation levels were, it's true, consistently two or three times higher than background but, at this point in my research, I knew how little that meant. It was about as radioactive as our medicine cabinet. When the Geiger counter ate through its batteries we didn't replace them.

Every week that summer, my children and I returned to the man-made wetlands, the little pocket of artificial wildness where mating swans now guarded their bright white eggs, each one the size of a baseball, kept safe in a nest embroidered with torn bits of blue plastic and chocolate wrappers. From here, we could just about see the site of the buried containment cell, though, in truth, we did not dwell on it. The cygnets were born at the end of summer, six of them, gray and fluffy, tottering around and falling down, climbing all over one other. We had to believe they were healthy. We gave them each a name.

Postscript

In February 2024, the City of Halle finally erected Erich Gadde's noticeboard in Ammendorf, acknowledging the history of this "Lost Place." The council also agreed to install four groundwater-testing stations around the former Orgacid site. In June 2024, Erich was diagnosed with prostate cancer. He continues to work on his list, which now has seventy-one names.

Over WhatsApp, Metin sent me pictures from the ceremony to mark the eighty-seventh anniversary of the massacres in Dersim. He was among those throwing roses into the Munzur, turning the river red.

Author's Note

This book touches on a number of complex subjects about which I am an expert in none. I'm thankful for the guidance of the many specialists who have helped me. All remaining errors are my own. While the events described are nonfiction and entirely based on my reading and interviews, I have taken significant liberties with the chronology of my own research for the sake of narrative progression and have dramatized moments in Siegfried's and Elisabeth's lives. In the Dersim chapter, some names and identifying details have been changed.

For references and a select bibliography, go to joedunthorne.com /childrenofradium.

Acknowledgments

As I hope is clear from the text, most of the significant discoveries I learned in writing this book were pointed out to me by other people. Below is an incomplete list of those to whom I owe gratitude for sharing their knowledge and expertise: Professor Taner Akçam; Gürdal Aksoy; Metin Albaslan, Jaclynn Ashly and Kerem; Ernie Althoff; Christian Becker at the Oranienburg City Archive; Frank Becker, Andrea Hohmeyer, and Ralf Peters at the Evonik archive; Clara Belessiotis-Richards; Juliane Busch; Paul Charman; Peter Cherry; Professor Robert Chilcott; everyone at the Dersim History and Culture Center; Tim Drayton; Cristal Duhaime; Martina Evans; Moradi Faraidoun; Wolfram Fischer; Ella Frears; Erich Gadde; Tanja Goldbecher; Matt Greene; Ernst Grube and Helga Hanusa; Professor Dr. Şaduman Halici; Mohammed Hanif; Jo Heygate at Pages Bookshop; Judith Hirsch-Rosenberg, Jason Oberlander, and Evelyne Oberlander; Lily E. Hirsch; Dr. Cristina Hohenlohe; Ali Ekber Kaya; Gerhard Keiper at the Political Archive of the Federal Foreign Office, Berlin; Kate Kilalea; Sandra Lipner; Susann List; Martin Luchterhandt at the Landesarchiv, Berlin; Elisabeth Macneal; David McDowall; Eleanor McDowall and Alan Hall at Falling Tree; Marta Medvešek; Rick Minnich; Professor Stephen Mitchell; Sylvia Naylor at the National Archives, Washington; Kaspar Nürnberg at the Aktives Museum; Philip Oltermann; Dr. Lisa Pine; Aubrey Pomerance and everyone at the Jewish Museum, Berlin; Ellen Presser at the Jewish Cultural Center, Munich; Caroline Pretty; Professor Johannes Preuss; Ernst Reimann; Nilüfer Saltik, Cemal Taş, and everyone at Kalan Music; Dr. Florian Schmaltz; Dr. Alexander von Schwerin; Michael Simonson at the Leo Baeck Institute; Gwen Speeth at the Houghton Library, Harvard; Johannes Streckenbach; Martina Voigt; and Lewis Watkins and Maria Sécio for breaking their phones with OCR scanning.

Thanks to everyone who worked on this book: Hermione Thompson, Ruby Fatimilehin, and Simon Prosser at Hamish Hamilton; Emily Polson, Valerie Steiker, and Colin Harrison at Scribner; Kathrin Liedtke at Berlin Verlag; and my agents, Georgia Garrett and Yasmin McDonald. Thanks to the Royal Literary Fund for their financial support when it was most needed. Thanks to my translator, Lena Kraus, who provided clean translations derived from badly lit phone photos of German documents written in sideways handwriting, often at short notice.

Special thanks and apologies to my extended family, who have been more generous than I dared to hope. I'm grateful for conversations with my dad, my sisters, Alison and Des McKenna, Keith, Patricia, Ruth, Luke and Matthew Brander, Celia, Charles and Matthew Merzbacher, Rachel and Tony Kitzinger. Thanks and love to Maya, who supported me in countless ways, discussed chemical weapons at length, and looked after our children while I took a number of research trips or, as she might prefer to call them, vacations.

Extra special thanks and love to my mother. When I told her that she was going to be a fairly prominent figure in the narrative, the first thing she asked was whether she could remain anonymous. In the end we agreed to just call her "my mother."

About the Author

JOE DUNTHORNE is a novelist and poet. His debut novel, *Submarine*, was translated into fifteen languages and made into an award-winning film. His second novel, *Wild Abandon*, won the Royal Society of Literature's Encore Award. He is also the author of *The Adulterants* and *O Positive: Poems*. His work has been published in *The New York Times*, *The New York Review of Books*, *London Review of Books*, *The Paris Review*, *McSweeney's*, *Granta*, *The Guardian*, and *The Atlantic*. He was born in Wales and lives in London.